JOURNAL *of* MUSEUM E

VOLUME 33 ❧ NUMBER 3 ❧ FALL 2008

A PUBLICATION OF THE MUSEUM EDUCATION ROUNDTABLE

Institution Wide Interpretive Planning

ISBN 978-1-59874-806-2

Journal of Museum Education (ISSN: 1059-8650), is published three times yearly, in the Spring, Summer, and Fall, by Left Coast Press, Inc., in partnership with the Museum Education Roundtable. The journal publishes original papers on theory, training, and practice in the museum education field. Each issue focuses on a specific theme of interest to professional and informal museum educators, administrators, and practitioners.

Subscriptions: All subscription inquiries should be sent to Left Coast Press, Inc., at the address below, addressed to the attention of the Journal Manager. Institutional subscriptions may be purchased via check, VISA, MasterCard, or purchase order. All non-institutional subscriptions should be prepaid by personal check, VISA, or MasterCard. Make checks payable to Left Coast Press, Inc. Current prices are listed on the publisher's website, or may be obtained by contacting the publisher at the address below. Payment in U.S. dollars only.

International Orders and Shipping: Add $15.00 per year for postage outside the United States.

Claims: Claims for missing copies will be honored for up to 12 months after date of publication. Missing copies due to losses in transit can be replaced pending availability of reserve stock.

Change of Address: Please notify the publisher six weeks in advance of address changes. Send old address label along with new address to ensure proper identification, and specify name of journal. *Postmaster:* Send all change of address to Left Coast Press, Inc., *Journal of Museum Education,* 1630 N. Main Street, #400, Walnut Creek, CA 94596.

Advertising: Current rates and specifications can be obtained by contacting the Journals Manager, Left Coast Press, Inc., at the address below.

Back issues: Back issues are available through Left Coast Press, Inc., at the address below.

Copyright Permission: For reprint permission requests please contact the publisher, Left Coast Press, Inc., at the address below.

Submission Guidelines: The *Journal of Museum Education* (JME) welcomes the submission of original papers on theory, training and practice in the museum education field, tailored to the theme of each issue. All manuscripts are subject to peer review by knowledgeable scholars and professional practitioners and, if accepted, may be subject to revision. Materials submitted to *JME* should not be under consideration by other publishers, nor should they be previously published in any form. For details on upcoming issue themes, manuscript composition, size, formatting, etc., please consult the Left Coast Press web site (www.lcoastpress.com) for journal submission guidelines. Reference style should conform to the Chicago Manual of Style, 15th edition. Non-conforming manuscripts will be returned to the author(s) for revision. Electronic submissions should include a cover note, article abstract, original article, short author(s) biography, and copies of any illustrations.

Send manuscript correspondence to Elizabeth Maurer, Editor, *Journal of Museum Education,* phone (571) 247-7155, email: JMuseEd@gmail.com.

Production and Composition by Detta Penna, Penna Design, Abbotsford, British Columbia

Printed in the United States of America

Left Coast Press, Inc.
1630 N. Main Street, #400
Walnut Creek, CA 94596
phone and fax (925) 935-3380
email journals@lcoastpress.com, web www.lcoastpress.com

"The purpose of a[n]...Institution-wide Interpretive Plan...is to define or articulate the intellectual framework that connects the mission of an organization and its collections with the needs and interests of its audiences."
(Comprehensive Interpretive Plans: A Framework
of Questions, Marianna Adams and Judy Koke)

In our first conversations on this topic, the guest editors and I discussed the differences between interpretive planning for programs and interpretive planning on an institutional level. Museum educators are accustomed to writing interpretive plans that set goals for the visitor experience, drawing upon content and collections to support the message and using innovative techniques to engage people in the museum experience. I wondered how an institution wide plan went beyond program planning. As Hudson Hill and Wild Czajkowski explain ("Transformation and Interpretation: What is the Museums Educator's Role?"), institution wide interpretive planning involves more than developing a strategic plan. It's an interdisciplinary approach whose end goal is to promote more dynamic interaction between visitors and objects. It's an area where educators have the credentials, passion, and ability to lead change.

It's a natural step to extend the techniques of planning for a program to planning for the entire institution. It's a big idea, really, and radical when you think about it: get everyone at the museum to develop a plan that will guide every aspect of the museum's mission from collections, to programming, to the web site, to exhibitions. However, it is a challenging proposition. How can an institution put aside departmental divisions to develop a plan?

At a time when many museums are rethinking their relevancy and relationships with audiences, institution wide interpretive planning puts educators at the center of decision making by drawing upon their leadership skills and audience-focused outlook to transform the museum experience. It's a process that can be applied to any museum regardless of subject matter or size. I would encourage you to draw inspiration from the examples and techniques that are profiled in this issue.

Liz Maurer

Elizabeth L. Maurer is the Director of Operations for the National Museum of Crime & Punishment in Washington, DC.

JOURNAL *of* MUSEUM EDUCATION

A PUBLICATION OF THE MUSEUM EDUCATION ROUNDTABLE

Editor
ELIZABETH MAURER
Director of Operations
The National Museum of Crime & Punishment

Institution Wide Interpretive Planning

Guest Editors
JUDY KOKE
Deputy Director of Education and Public Programming,
The Art Gallery of Ontario, Canada

MARIANNA ADAMS
President, Audience Focus, Inc.

Editorial Advisors

AMELIA CHAPMAN, Curator of Education, Pacific Asia Museum

CYNTHIA COPELAND, Principal, The OutSourced Muse

MARK HOWELL, Director of Education,
American Civil War Center at Historic Tredegar

LYNN MCRAINEY, Director of Education, Chicago History Museum

SUSAN SPERO, Associate Professor, Museum Studies,
John F. Kennedy University

SCOTT WINTERROWD, Assistant Curator of Education,
Meadows Museum at Southern Methodist University

Outside Readers

ERIK HOLLAND, Interpretive Program Associate-Historic Sites
Minnesota Historical Society

CYNTHIA ROBINSON, Director of Museum Studies, Tufts University

The *Museum Education Roundtable* (MER) is a nonprofit organization based in Washington, DC, dedicated to enriching and promoting the field of Museum Education. Through publications, programs, and communication networks, *MER* fosters professionalism, encourages leadership, scholarship, and research in museum-based learning, and advocates the inclusion and application of museum-based learning in the general education arena. For more information on MER and its activities, please contact via email at info@mer-online.com, or on the web at www.mer-online.org. Members receive the *Journal of Museum Education* as a benefit of membership. Write to *MER* at PO Box 15727, Washington, DC 20003.

Our Full Share of Delight and Content

Judy Koke & Marianna Adams

There is an old children's poem that comes to mind when thinking about the potential of the museum experience. It goes something like this: "Jill came from the fair with her pennies all spent. She'd had her full share of delight and content." In our experience, we've found that museum practitioners dearly want their visitors to feel delight and content after visiting the museum. We know that it happens for some people but not all and so we constantly tinker with exhibitions and programs to increase the likelihood that more and more visitors will have "peak" or transformative experiences in the museum. In this time of economic insecurity the competition for visitors will only be more intense and tinkering around the edges will no longer be enough. The articles and case studies in this issue support the idea that only substantial institutional shifts in thinking about the visitor experience can create a level of delight and content that makes a real difference in visitors' lives.

The issue begins with Cheryl Meszaros' erudite illumination of the concepts of Hans-Georg Gadamer as they frame a philosophical foundation for thinking about interpretation in "Un/Familiar." She challenges us to see understanding as "part of an ongoing process, rather than an act that is completed." Within this process we are invited to re-examine the notions of prejudice and authority as they operate in the museum for staff and visitors alike.

Judy Koke's article on the role of comprehensive interpretive plans as the "The Next Step in Visitor Centeredness and Business Success" grounds this issue in the recent history of the museum field. She provides a brief overview of how this issue emerged from our professional practice and how it contributes to the success of the museum as a business.

Shiralee Hudson Hill and Jennifer Wild Czajkowski, in "Transformation and Interpretation: What is the museum educators role?" provide insight into how the recent and innovative interpretive planning process at the Detroit Institute of Arts and the Art Gallery of Ontario resulted in a new role for museum educators. Drawing on bell hooks' approach to the benefits of working from the margins, this article examines how educators can lead transformative change.

Three brief case studies serve to illustrate the variety of ways that interpretive planning has evolved and the lessons learned along the way. In "How a Museum Discovered the Transforming Power of Play," Scott Eberle recounts the Strong National Museum of Play's search for its essence where joy and enlightenment live affectionately side-by-side. James Hakala in "Building Balance" identifies internal and external factors that stimulate the development of an institution-wide interpretive plan, stressing the development of a storyline that links the museum, objects, and the community. Beth Schneider, in "An Interpretive Master Plan at the Museum of Fine Arts, Houston," looks back at the interpretive planning process over the past decade, extracting valuable lessons learned along the way.

Because comprehensive interpretive plans are relatively new in the museum field this issue concludes with three valuable resources to help practitioners begin their own process. Marcella Wells reports on "An Evaluation of the Effectiveness of National Park Service Interpretive Planning" where she led a meta-study of fourteen interpretive plans. She articulates the components of effective plans and clearly points out areas in these plans where practitioners often fall short. The guest editors contributed an article, "Comprehensive Interpretive Plans: A Framework of Questions," to guide discussions in your museum. Currently there is no one model or recipe for developing such plans, and some maintain that the process should always stay fluid and responsive, so our framework of questions seeks to offer sufficient structure to guide you along the process. Finally, Jes Koepfler in "Just Do It: Resources for Interpretive Planning" offers a well-researched annotated bibliography of articles, books, and websites to assist you in the interpretive planning process.

Marianna Adams is president of Audience Focus, Inc. which supports museums, cultural organizations, and other informal learning environments in the development of unique life-enriching experiences for diverse audiences. Dr. Adams specializes in professional development for museum practitioners to learn how to conduct their own evaluation, in designing visitor studies that assist museums in better understanding and service audiences, and in facilitating interpretive planning efforts at museums. She can be contacted at Marianna@audiencefocus.com.

Judy Koke is the Deputy Director of Education and Public Programming for the Art Gallery of Ontario in Toronto, Canada. In this capacity she leads the interpretive planning and visitor research functions for the museum. Formerly a Senior Researcher at the Institute for Learning Innovation, she has extensive background in research and evaluation and in integrating visitor input into museum planning. Previously, the in-house evaluator at the Denver Museum of Nature and Science for six years, Judy was later the Assistant Director of the University of Colorado Museum of Natural History. She has taught in several graduate Museum Studies Programs and has published widely on youth programs, gender differences in science attitudes and specific audience segments.

Un/Familiar

Cheryl Meszaros

History does not belong to us, we belong to it.
Gadamer, 1990, p. 276

Abstract   What I put forward here is that the interpretative practices of the museum, whether they take the form of exhibitions, education programs, written texts or digital productions, are fashioned by relationships between the familiar and unfamiliar, which in turn both shape and are shaped by human understanding in general. The development of a new field of practice—interpretive planning—is an encouraging recognition of the centrality and the complexity of these relationships.

Interpretation—it is such a convivial concept! Full of gracious hospitality, it welcomes all of its old and familiar friends, the quiet and unobtrusive meaning-making routines that run in the background of our lives, telling us that this is hot, this is pink, this a door and this is how to use the stairs without much effort or thought. In this respect, interpretation has a certain mature ease, a quiet conventionality wrought from tradition and repetition; it knows how to figure things, what to make of things, and when to take action. Yet interpretation also has a "wild side." It embraces the profoundly unfamiliar; it comes to the fore and requires attention when it stands in the presence of fantastically ancient things, spectacularly new things, exceedingly complicated things, radically "other" things, and it positively sparkles in the company of the profound, playful, and ambiguous phenomena we call poetry, literature, and art. These unfamiliar and unruly things compel us to interpret them. They are the convivial host of interpretation, its playmate, mother, buddy, teacher, disciplinarian—its new friend. The unfamiliar things, in their robust novelty and in their stalwart sameness, offer us the opportunity to encounter interpretation itself, to heed the elusive, shadowy repertoires of meaning-making that shape the thoughts, opinions, ideas, and actions we call our own. The unfamiliar things—these are the things that museums and galleries are made of.

What I put forward here is that the interpretative practices of the museum, whether they take the form of exhibitions, education programs, written texts, or digital productions, are fashioned by relationships between the familiar and unfamiliar, which in turn both shape and are shaped by human understanding in general. The development of a new field of practice—interpretive planning—is an encouraging recognition of the centrality and the complexity of these relationships. That this field is developing so rapidly and that it has increasing power to shape the interpretive mandate of the museum, makes it all the more urgent to attend to this central question of the passages between the familiar and the unfamiliar. Bill Brown addresses a similar mechanism of passage in his discussion of the distinctions between things and objects. Things, he says, are unnamable, unintelligible, vaguely apprehended; e.g., that thing over there.[1] Objects, by comparison, are interpretable, meaningful; they are things that have been made into evidence and facts. For Brown, things come to exist as objects only in relation to a society that values and interprets them. Similarly, for the museum philosopher Hilde Hein, objecthood results from multilevel acts of attention by individuals and social groups who imbue it with meaning through sanctioned structures of reference.[2] What I stress here is that the passage from unfamiliar to familiar is not a simple one-way passage. As such, it cannot be instrumentalized into normative and prescriptive representations of interpretation. Further, although I do not posit that there is one, or even one cluster, of correct definitions or practices of interpretation, or ways to deal with the unfamiliar, I do maintain that there is a discourse of interpretation, a long dialogue with the great thinkers of meaning-making that is important to consider at this moment when new practices of interpretive planning are forming in the museum.

How to deal with the unfamiliar, the mysterious and the unknown is perhaps one of the most persistent and productive thematics in the history of meaning-making. This central motif of culture has generated fabulous and familiar myths, constructed the master narratives that structure beliefs, convictions and certainty, birthed the sciences and humanities, spawned new disciplines, fuelled furious disciplinary wars and yielded a plethora of new methods and processes by which we come to understand the unfamiliars—God, nature, truth, history, self, other.[3] Here I will focus on two concepts from the work of Hans-Georg Gadamer—prejudice and authority—and examine how these concepts can shed light on understanding interpretation differently.

GADAMER

Hans-Georg Gadamer (1900–2002) was a continental philosopher whose work addressed the question of how to understand the nature of human understanding. He is recognized as one of the key figures in the reshaping of hermeneutics theory.[4] Until the early twentieth century, hermeneutics (theories of interpretation) was occupied with methodical expositions of the rules governing interpretation.[5] Gadamer recast this approach by thinking interpretation through phenomenology, which, very simply put, is a reflective study of meaning as it is experienced by the first-person singular. This hybrid project of looking at both the rules and the variable experiences of interpretation is known as philosophical hermeneutics.[6] Yet within this project, Gadamer did not direct his effort toward teaching people how to interpret as such; rather, he sought to explore how interpretation is practiced. What Gadamer found, though, is that the practice of interpretation—for example, *my* experience of becoming familiar with something that was unfamiliar—is intimately bound not only to *my* past, but to *a* past that precedes and exceeds me.[7]

This broad shift in viewpoint from a prescriptive endeavor (defining the rules, steps, and strategies of interpretation) to a descriptive one (addressing how interpretation takes place rather than simply listing what interpretations arise) offers a valuable model for the museum. This changed perspective asks, perhaps even demands, a focus on what occurs prior to the interpretive act. It questions what "familiars" lurk behind the interpretive plan, before the big ideas, story lines, methods, strategies, flow charts, and learning outcomes.[8] Moreover, this shift concentrates attention on interpretation itself, asking how to apprehend the unfamiliar and to acknowledge the familiar. Many different disciplines within the physical, social, and human sciences continue to have a stake in this bewilderingly question of how an event of meaning takes place. The hope for interpretive planning is that it has the mandate to explore interpretation as such, to bring different ways of comprehending the project of human understanding into the museum. This is a timely opportunity, and a time-sensitive one. Over the past few years, there has been a veritable explosion of new museum scholars, researchers and writers who have taken up this project of recognizing and moving beyond familiar education and outcome-based strategies, to rethink the project of interpretation in the museum.[9] What was once the radically unfamiliar and poignantly unwelcome, that is, the theorization of interpretation from philosophical, literary, informatic, and hermeneutic perspectives, is now becoming, if not familiar, at least discernible in the museum. The question is how to welcome these new acquaintances into the museum. I suggest that we greet them one by one, and along the way perhaps befriend a few, who in turn will bring their colleagues and associates to the museum. With that premise, I now turn to Gadamer's ideas of prejudice and authority.

PREJUDICE

In his most renowned book, *Truth and Method*, Gadamer queries how the humanities (as a form of understanding) become so impoverished and, further, how the humanities' claim to know something true came to be measured by a standard foreign to it — namely the methodological thinking of the modern sciences.[10] In this context, he examines the role that pre-judgment, or what he calls prejudice, plays in understanding. He disagrees with the negative connotations of prejudice fostered by the experimental fervor of the natural sciences, particularly the idea that prejudice clouds the judgment of pure reason and limits our freedom to think differently.[11] Instead, he proposes that far from closing off understanding, our prejudices are themselves what open us to understanding: they are the preconditions of understanding. Prejudices are part of the larger social structures that evolve historically within communities and into which we are socialized and shaped through a matrix of language, practice and individual community and corporate experiences.[12] These preconditions precede us. They are the generative force of the hermeneutic circle, providing a picture of the whole — however vague and changeable — through which the parts begin to make sense. They offer us, for example, a certain idea of what a novel is before we begin interpreting a specific novel, an idea of what a museum is about before we cross its threshold. In contrast with the traditional hermeneutic theory, though, Gadamer rejects the idea that understanding is achieved by gaining access to some inner realm of subjective meaning.[13] Further, since understanding is part of an ongoing process, rather than an act that is completed, he also rejects the idea that there is any final outcome to understanding. It is on this basis that

Gadamer argues against the suggestion that there is a method or technique for achieving understanding.

For museums, it is hardly news that people come to the museum with prejudgments, with all of their familiar routines playing in the background, and then proceed to interpret objects and exhibitions from there. This is the philosophical underpinning of constructivist learning theory that constitutes the mainstay of museum educational practices.[14] Further, it comprises the material evidence sought by audience researchers who, for example, track the effect of exhibitions on specific entrance narratives or listen in on conversations that explicate these shifts.[15] But although Gadamer would not deny that people make their own meaning from their prejudices and prior knowledge, he is after something more subtle. He is trying to account for how prejudices are established, how traditions become authoritative. More importantly, he is asking how it is possible to change the authoritative traditions of meaning-making and how we can distinguish between those authorities that are useful and those that are restrictive. Hilde Hein takes up something similar when she says that unless the museum goes beyond the fact of experiential individuality to investigate its vast penumbral hinterland, there is little value in being the occasion of experience. Meaning, she insists, is not generated by the individual alone.[16] But how do we get to this penumbral hinterland, this home of the familiar? Gadamer offers us one route that comes in the form of a rethink of the concept of authority.

AUTHORITY

Gadamer argues that over time, many of the routines of meaning-making become familiar to the point of being second nature and subsequently become the unquestioned rules, the silent but insistent traditions that appear as our own thoughts, ideas and opinions. Think, for instance, of the sheer volume of subliminal routines that run under a statement such as "That's not art, I could do that!" The museum is deeply complicit in sustaining and valorizing these authorities. It does this through exhibitions and programs that promote certain kinds of narratives and ways of thinking and certain forms of compliance and dissent. The museum executes this authorizing function most powerfully and insidiously in what it allows to go unnoticed, unrecognized, and unacknowledged. This was the case, for example, with the colonizing narratives of the early twentieth-century museum. One could easily chart the recent history of the museum in terms of its gradual recognition of the impact and implications of its own authority, followed by moves to either exploit its authority in order to grow the coffers, audiences, and franchises or, conversely and frequently simultaneously, its attempts to diffuse and relocate authority, assigning it to source communities, target audiences or the underrepresented, or simply turning it over to individual meaning-makers. Gadamer offers a fresh way to think about authority. He posits that authority is not always necessarily oppressive or exploitative, it is not only or always "power over." Rather, authority is also, and perhaps more significantly, the acknowledgment of knowledge. Authority has to do with knowledge, not obedience, and, like respect, it is earned over time.

How the museum recuperates and rehabilitates this more productive idea of authority—how it acknowledges its own knowledge—is both the mandate and the challenge of the recent turn toward interpretation in the museum. How can the museum befriend and embrace content knowledge garnered from deep within a discipline, especially at a moment when disciplinary knowledge is suspect, and interdisciplinary knowledge is perceived as superficial?[17] How can the museum nurture and sustain content knowledge from which to forge a few truly compelling and poignant sentences or gestures that direct us to interpretation? I am speaking here of the content knowledge traditionally held by curators, academics, and researchers whose job it is to possess disciplinary knowledge, to be aware of traditions and methods that shape it, and to know when to honor those traditions and when to challenge them. The celebrated "trustworthiness" of the museum, it seems to me, adheres in this deep and rich content knowledge. Acknowledging, honoring, and sharing this knowledge—"telling" visitors something gripping about the old, new, and other things in the museum's collections—hardly constitutes a closure of interpretation. It does not impose authority over others, it is not an act of intellectual elitism, and it most certainly does not offend visitors' right to make whatever interpretation they like about the things in the museum.[18] Rather, this form of sharing deep content knowledge is a warm invitation to enter into dialogue with the unfamiliar; it is the warn introduction to a stranger and an opening to understanding. Understanding, Gadamer declares, "lets itself be addressed by tradition."[19]

UN/FAMILIARS

Gadamer tells us that it is the tyranny of hidden prejudices that makes us deaf to what speaks to us in tradition.[20] Interpretive planning, it seems, is poised to play a vital role in the rehabilitation of the impoverished notions of authority, tradition, and prejudice that can open the dialogue between the familiar and the unfamiliar, between the visitor, objects, and the museum. Yet the question has been — and, I think, remains — in what direction does this dialogue flow? Although dialogue connotes a convivial to and fro, it rarely manifests that. When does the familiar, in the form of individual experience, or what I have elsewhere called the "whatever" interpretation,[21] work to consume, ignore or simply snub the unfamiliar? When does the unfamiliar institutionalize itself in methods that, as Gadamer and others have suggested, only work to reproduce the impoverished side of authority? Particularly in these formative moments, interpretive planning has the potential and the power to undertake and to model more equitable dialogues with history, authority, and prejudice. Similar to the way that Viktor Shklovsky describes how poetic language defamiliarizes the familiar, helping us pay attention to language that is otherwise invisible, interpretive planning is in a position to help visitors pay heed to routines of meaning-making.[22] This form of interpretation would not work to make interpretation seamless; it would not ask: What are your opinions? Rather, it would ask, as Nealon and Searls Giroux do: Where do the thoughts, ideas, opinions and experience that we call our own come from?[23]

In this dialogue of understanding inspired by Gadamer, prejudices — as an occurrence of tradition — come to the fore, both in the role they play in opening up what is to be understood and in the way they themselves become evident in that process. As our prejudices become apparent to us, they can also become the focus of questioning.[24] It is from this place of inquiry, forged from deep within tradition, that we become capable of modifying those traditions in meaningful ways. It is here that we are reacquainted with old familiar routines, and where we can greet the unfamiliar with generosity.

Notes

1. Bill Brown, "Thing Theory," in *Things,* ed. Bill Brown (Chicago: University of Chicago Press, 2004), 4-5.
2. Hilda Hein, *Public Art: Thinking Museums Differently* (Lanham MD: AltaMira Press, 2006), 64.
3. Margorie Garber, *Academic Instincts* (Princeton: Princeton University Press, 2001).
4. Robert Dostal, *The Cambridge Companion to Gadamer* (Cambridge: Cambridge University Press, 2002).
5. Jean Grondin, *Sources of Hermeneutic* (Albany NY: State University of New York Press, 1995).
6. David Hiley, James Bohman, and Richard Schusterman, eds. *The Interpretive Turn: Philosophy, Science, Culture* (Ithaca and London: Cornell University Press 1991).

7. Hans-Georg Gadamar, *Truth and Method* (New York: Crossroads, 2004).

8. Beverly Serrell, *Judging Exhibitions: A Framework for Assessing Excellence* (Walnut Creek CA.: Left Coast Press, 2006). Eileaen Hooper-Greenhill, *Museums and Education: Purpose, Pedagogy, Performance* (New York: Routledge, 2007).

9. Sharon Macdonald and Paul Basu, eds. *Exhibition Experiments* (Oxford: Blackwell, 2007). Ivan Karp and others, eds. *Museum Frictions: Public Cultures/Global Transformations* (Durham: Duke University Press, 2006). Peter Weibel and Andrea Buddensieg, eds. *Contemporary Art and the Museum* (Karlsruhe: Centre for Art and Media, 2007).

10. Gadamar, 2004.

11. Hans-Georg Gadamer, "The Discrediting of Prejudice by the Enlightenment and Rehabilitation of Authority and Tradition," in *The Hermeneutics Reader*, ed. Kurt Mueller-Vollmer (New York: Continuum Publishing Company, 1994), 276.

12. B. Wachterhauser, "Getting It Right: Relativism, Realism, and Truth," in *The Cambridge Companion to Gadamer*, ed. Robert Dostal (Cambridge: Cambridge University Press, 2002).

13. Wilhelm Dilthey, *Selected Writings* (Cambridge: Cambridge University Press, 1979). Friedrich Schleiermacher, *Hermeneutics and Criticism and Other Writings* (Cambridge: Cambridge University Press, 1998).

14. George Hein, *Learning in the Museum* (London: Routledge, 1998). John Falk, *Learning from Museums: Visitor Experiences and the Making of Meaning* (Lanham MD: AltaMira Press, 2000).

15. Gaea Leinhadt, Kevin Crowley and Karen Knutson, eds. *Learning Conversations in Museums.* (Mahwah NJ: Lawrence Erlbaum 2002).

16. Hein, 64.

17. Ibid, 64.

18. Cheryl Meszaros, "Now THAT is evidence: Tracking Down the Evil 'Whatever Interpretation'," *Visitor Studies Today 9* no. 3 (2006): 10–12.

19. Gadamer, 2004, p. 282.

20. Gadamer, 2004.

21. Cheryl Meszaros, "Interpretation in the Reign of the 'Whatever'," *MUSE: Journal of the Canadian Museums Association* 25 no. 1, (2007): 16–29.

22. Paul Steiner, "Russian Formalism" In The Cambridge History of Literary Criticism, Volume 8 From Formalism to Poststructuralism, ed. Ramen Selden) Cambridge University press, 1995), 11-32.

23. Jeffrey Nealon and Susan Searls Giroux *The Theory Toolbox: Critical Concepts for the Humanities, Arts and Social Sciences.* Lanham: Rowman & Littlefield, 2003), 4.

24. Elliot Kai-Kee, "Gallery Teaching as Guided Interpretation: Museum Education and Practice and Hermeneutic Theory," in *From Periphery to Center: Art Museum in the Twenty-first Century*, ed. P. Villeneuve (Reston, VA, National Art Education Association 2007).

Dr. Cheryl Meszaros teaches in the Museum Studies Program at the University of Toronto, Canada. She specializes in museum interpretation, hermeneutic theory and educational practices and consults in these areas. She is the recent recipient of a J. Paul Getty Museum Scholar Grant in Los Angles, California. She was Head of Public Programs at the Vancouver Art Gallery, British Columbia for over ten years and a periodic Lecturer and Adjunct Professor of Art Education at the University of British Columbia and a Lecturer at the Emily Carr College of Art and Design in Vancouver.

Comprehensive Interpretive Plans
The Next Step in Visitor Centeredness and Business Success?

Judy Koke

Abstract   For this author, the in-depth conversation about Comprehensive Interpretive Plans (CIP) began at an AAM Task Force meeting in May of 2004. Building on that initial discussion, the author explores the reasons, costs and benefits of engaging in the CIP development process, and makes the case for the museum field to develop proficiency in this practice as the next step in visitor-centeredness and business success.

One of the functions of the American Association of Museums (AAM) is to accredit museums according to a set of published standards in order to establish the professionalism of their practice, staff, and facility for the museum community and for external stakeholders.

> AAM Accreditation is a widely recognized seal of approval that brings national recognition to a museum for its commitment to excellence, accountability, high professional standards, and continued institutional improvement.[1]

In 2003 and 2004, AAM considered the possible addition of Institution-wide Interpretive Plans as part of the accreditation process.[2] In May of 2004, the American Association of Museums sponsored a two day Task Force on Comprehensive Interpretive Planning to gather a group of experienced professionals to articulate and compile the field's understanding of this process. Some sixty professionals from thirty diverse American museums[3] actively engaged in this process gathered to articulate the development and contents of an effective Comprehensive Interpretive Plan.

The AAM Task Force developed a working definition of a Comprehensive Interpretive Plan (CIP) as:

> A written document that outlines the stories and messages the museum wants to convey through a variety of media such as exhibits, programming, and publications. It may include the institution's interpretive philosophy, educational goals, and target audiences.

From this overarching, foundational plan can be developed supporting plans that describe individual programs, galleries, or exhibitions. The CIP should be rooted in the organization's mission and strategic plan and be interconnected with the Collections plan. (For more information on the AAM workshop see www.aam-us.org.) Beyond this working definition, however, what emerged from the colloquium was the finding that, while everyone thought this was an important topic, our profession held no shared understanding of either what comprised an Comprehensive Interpretive Plan or the best process to develop one.[4]

Does this matter? Why should our field feel compelled to become proficient in this practice? If and when we become fluent in this exercise, why should AAM require such a plan as part of the demonstration of a museum's professional capacity? Part of the answer to these questions lies in the fairly recent movement of our organizations to define their "public value".[5] Progress in the field of visitor studies and evaluation has recently encouraged museums—in addition to determining success by measuring specific program or exhibition outcomes—to consider how individual programs further the organizational mission. Mission statements are, however, often grand and expansive and are usually not written to be easily measurable. Institution-wide, or Comprehensive Interpretive Plans, provide the intellectual framework that connects an organization's mission and collections with the needs of its audiences, thus describing an organization's unique role in the life of a community. In addition, in 1993 with the publication of *Excellence and Equity*, museums proclaimed themselves as institutions of public education. Despite this fact, AAM accreditation currently does not require an education plan to compliment the strategic and collections plans required for accreditation and museums are not in the practice of developing such a plan to define their public education role.

Comprehensive Interpretive Plans are an exercise in looking outward and into the future. CIPs describe how public offerings such as exhibitions and programs (in-house and outreach) work together to build the organization's desired relationship with its audiences and its active participation in its community. Further, a Comprehensive Interpretive Plan builds strong community relationships through transparency and explicit purpose and decision making. All of this is not accomplished without cost; CIPs require a significant investment of staff time, particularly when developed in an inclusive manner. Most of us, all too familiar with the time invested in strategic planning and/or departmental planning, are inclined to groan at the thought of developing yet another document. However, our profession is slowly beginning to recognize the importance of this work and to develop the processes to create such plans effectively and efficiently.

CLARITY OF PURPOSE

Often, the need for a CIP originates during the process of strategic planning. While engaged in the process of articulating what it is that they do, museums move beyond defining their collections and research agendas to how their publics connect to that work.

Museum workers have a long history of developing strong interpretive plans for specific programs or exhibitions that detail visitor outcomes, main messages, and big ideas. What they have been less successful at detailing however, is their overall message or purpose in a community. The Strong National Museum of Play utilized its need to rethink its role and purpose to develop such a plan that, beyond public offerings, unified the institutional purpose and resulted in a transformed institution as outlined in the case study that follows in this issue. Similarly, the University of Colorado Museum of Natural History and Anthropology felt a strong need to define itself and its role as different from its nearby and larger neighbor, the Denver Museum of Nature and Science, and found the development of a CIP to be the vehicle that articulated that difference.

The Detroit Institute of Arts (DIA) engaged in a massive construction project to update an aging building and saw the reinstallation as an opportunity to completely re-think what was happening with visitors. As Jennifer Wild Czajkowski, Associate Educator for Interpretation (and an author in this journal), suggests:

For the DIA, a Comprehensive Interpretive Plan was part of the answer to a number of questions we posed about who we were as an institution.

How can we use our collection to make the museum a more useful and relevant place for our audience? How can we broaden our audience and help more people see that art can play a role in the way they think about and understand themselves, their neighbors and the world? How can we create an environment where visitors can find personal meaning in art?

As staff participated in CIP work and began to really understand what it might take to be a visitor-centered institution, it became apparent that "we had to change the way we did business and the way we thought about our relationship with visitors....You might say it gave us a better focus and perhaps a stronger sense of identity."[6]

In each of these examples there was a desire for clarity of purpose, both for working together as a staff and, equally important, for communicating to audiences what the role of the museum was or could be in the community. Each of these organizations desired to be a more vibrant institution with an increased ability to attract audiences and funding. Developing a CIP, an explicit description of the role they were determined to play in the life of the community, was a strong step in the direction of success.

SHARED LANGUAGE AND SPACE

Prior to the reinstallation, the DIA routinely invested significant resources in special exhibitions, often with innovative interpretative plans; however, the outstanding permanent collection was displayed with minimal interpretation. Internal visitor studies indicated that very few visitors could make sense of it. In order to provide a high-quality experience supporting true connections between the audience and the collection, the DIA realized it would be necessary to integrate community input with organization knowledge and recent visitor research and evaluation findings. A centralized plan that incorporated recent research and visitor studies findings ensured that critical ideas and strategies were applied evenly and appropriately throughout the museum.

In 2006, the Art Gallery of Ontario (AGO) also became deeply involved in Comprehensive Interpretive Planning in conjunction with a major expansion. Kelly McKinley, the Richard and Elizabeth Currie Director of Education and Public Programming, described a change in work process and priorities at the AGO as a result of this process based on a new and shared description of the institution's desired relationship with the city. To accomplish the installation of 110 galleries, the cross divisional teams were required to invest significant time in developing a shared framework of values, called "Guiding Principles", that articulate the organization's broad understanding of diversity, responsiveness, participation, and learning as it can occur in the museum's galleries and outside the museum's walls. While individuals and departments still struggle to integrate this framework into practice, McKinley suggests this new, shared vocabulary also supports a more neutral space for the discussion of ideas. "It used to be that some people's language and ideas were significantly more privileged over others. As we all use the same language now there is more equality in idea generation and development. We see this as an opportunity as more ideas come from all kinds of places."[7] A shared framework can extend beyond those departments planning visitor learning experiences. CIPs can decrease the single-minded emphasis on exhibitions as visitor experiences as the broader staff discusses which stories are best told in which medium. If all staff members participate in the broad discussions of interpretive planning, across the entire organization, discussions follow about which messages are best delivered in an exhibition as opposed to the website, a publication, or a public program. This includes discussion of marketing and retail messages and how they might or might not reinforce key messages.

SUPPORTING CREATIVITY

One concern often voiced in response to the idea of a Comprehensive Interpretive Plan is that too strong a framework will inhibit the very creativity required to develop unique and compelling visitor experiences. While this concern was heard at many of the aforementioned institutions early in their processes, the organizations feel they have created CIPs that are flexible frameworks that keep the visitor at the center of the experience and suggest how to recognize and measure success. In the Museum of Fine Art Houston Case Study, Beth Schneider describes the role their Interpretive Master Plan took in redefining and measuring success. This focus on integrating a visitor-based definition of success required ongoing audience research, which in turn stimulated a wide variety of new ideas and approaches to interpretive work.

BUSINESS SUCCESS

The museum field in North America may be moving towards the development of Comprehensive Interpretive Plans not simply as good scholarship and professional rigor but also as a tool to support business success. In the spring of 2005, Harold and Susan Skamstead wrote "[T]o be successful each museum must emerge as a distinctive organization with a unique mission and vision that cannot be carried out better by another organization. It must be connected to its audiences, and it must be a trustworthy source of information, a place where anyone can come to learn, taking from the museum's messages those things that have value and relevance to their own lives."[8]

John Falk and Beverly Sheppard go further to advise that museums need to answer four key questions:

1. *Why do you exist?... Who is your public and what specific needs do they have that you are uniquely positioned to satisfy?*
2. *What assets do you bring to the table?*
3. *How will you forge and maintain partnerships with like minded organizations in the community in order to leverage your impact?*
4. *What is the unique combination of products and services you can provide to satisfy specific public needs and generate sufficient revenues to keep your doors open?*[9]

The development of a Comprehensive Interpretive Plan begins to answer those questions and supports the development and delivery of a clear, cohesive message that in turn supports transparency and inclusiveness. The plan can explain purpose and direction to both internal and external stakeholders, which, again, supports strong partnering with community groups. It sharpens the museum's focus and balances the museum in being visitor-centered as well as collections-centered. The plan encourages reflective practice on the part of the organization—a key action in learning organizations—and supports better decision making by including multiple stakeholders at the inception of planning. And possibly most importantly, by ensuring a shared belief system, a Comprehensive Interpretive Plan changes the focus of day-to-day efforts from what the museum is to what the museum wants to be.

Notes

1. From AAM website, April 13, 2008 www.aam-us.org
2. Alternatively called Institution-wide Interpretive Plans, Interpretive Master Plans, or Comprehensive Interpretive Plans, our field has not identified the preferred title and this article will use all three names interchangeably.
3. Museum—broadly—zoo, aquarium, etc.
4. For the purposes of this paper, an Institution-wide, or Comprehensive Interpretive plan is an overarching document that guides all the educational programming, outreach and visi-

tor experiences that museums, zoos, aquaria, nature parks and other free-choice learning environments offer.

5. Moore, Mark. *Creating Public Value: Strategic Management in Government* (Cambridge, Massachusetts: Harvard University Press, 1995)
Koster, E and J. Falk, "Maximizing the External Value of Museums" Curator 50:2 (Lanham, MD: AltaMira Press, 2007) 191-196.
Korn, R., "The Case for Holistic Intentionality" *Curator,* 50:2 (Lanham, MD: AltaMira Press, 2007) 255-264.
6. Personal Communication, March 2006.
7. Personal Communication, March 2006
8. Harold and Susan Skamstead, "In Search of the American Museum: Dreaming the Museum." *Museum News* 84,(March/April 2005): 53.
9. John H. Falk and Beverly K. Sheppard, *Thriving in the Knowledge Age: New Business Models for Museums and Other Cultural Institutions* (Lanham, MD: Rowman AltaMira, 2006), 20.

Judy Koke is the Deputy Director of Education and Public Programming for the Art Gallery of Ontario. In this capacity she leads the interpretive planning and visitor research functions for the museum. Formerly a Senior Researcher at the Institute for Learning Innovation, she has extensive background in research and evaluation and in integrating visitor input into museum planning. Previously, the in-house evaluator at the Denver Museum of Nature and Science for six years, Judy was later the Assistant Director of the University of Colorado Museum of Natural History. She has taught in several graduate Museum Studies Programs and has published widely on youth programs, gender differences in science attitudes and specific audience segments.

Transformation and Interpretation
What is the Museums Educator's Role?

Jennifer Wild Czajkowski and Shiralee Hudson Hill

Abstract This paper looks at how two art museums are striving to create relevant, dialogic gallery spaces where broader audiences can make meaning. Using the writings of theorist bell hooks[1] as the framework, it proposes museum educators' experiences working from the margins of their museums' hierarchical organizations is fundamental to their work in leading such transformative change. These ideas are discussed in relation to permanent collection reinstallations and major architectural projects at the Detroit Institute of Arts (DIA) and the Art Gallery of Ontario (AGO).

For many years, museums of all types have been engaged in an ideological shift toward considering visitors' ideas, needs, and experiences in their comprehensive planning efforts. The museum model has slowly been moving away from that of authoritative lecturer before a passive audience to that of a partner in dialogue with interested, engaged community members. This paper explores recent, intensive examples of this shift at two art institutions: the Detroit Institute of Arts (DIA) and the Art Gallery of Ontario (AGO). Both museums have been engaged in permanent collection reinstallations and major architectural projects meant to reinvent their relationships with visitors.[2] Education departments at both museums have been unusually influential in these projects.

Through the experiences of these two institutions, this paper also explores why art museum educators are often well-positioned to lead a museum's transformation into relevant and dialogic public spaces, positing that the traditional marginalization of educators in museums' strategic decision-making processes, and their long history of working with the formerly

Journal of Museum Education, Volume 33, Number 3, Fall 2008, pp. 255–264.

marginalized general public, may be key to their role in leading such change. It is hoped that by examining the particular characteristics of the changing art museum educators' role, educators at all types of museums will be inspired to take a critical look at their positions within museum hierarchies to see the opportunities that may exist.

NEW ROLES AND RESPONSIBILITIES

New institutional priorities have emerged as museum missions have shifted. Interpretation is increasingly being designed to facilitate dynamic, dialogic experiences that will ignite visitors' imaginations, ideas, and emotions and encourage self-reflection and social engagement. As a result, the departments responsible for interpretation and public programming have been impacted profoundly. In this context, interpretation can be defined as the ways that art, objects and ideas are presented to visitors in order to facilitate the visitor experience—noting that visitor experiences are far from being singular in nature.

Addressing these new priorities requires new expertise, organizational structures, and roles. In the past, curators have generally made all key decisions about art gallery installations; other staff members supported the curator's vision. With the current shift in direction at art museums, interdisciplinary teams of curators, educators, designers, evaluators, and project managers are being asked to collaboratively re-imagine gallery installations and exhibition programs. Increased understanding of diverse professional concerns, and compromise, rather than hierarchies and control, are their modus operandi.

To address the planning complexities associated with the development of more holistic and inclusive exhibition spaces, the role of interpretive planning has taken on new prominence at both the AGO and the DIA. Although professional development for interpretive planners varies, many cut their museum teeth in education departments. Perhaps for this reason, as well as the shared values between interpretive planning and education, many museum educators are being called upon to fulfill the role of interpretive planner in the exhibition development process. This has been the case at the DIA and to some extent the AGO.

Within this new team environment, is it surprising that staff from museum education departments are playing a leading role in developing visitor-centered interpretation and more visitor-friendly galleries? Not at all. In fact it is more appropriate than some museum managers may realize, as the projects in Detroit and Toronto demonstrate.

PROJECTS AT THE DIA AND THE AGO

In 2002, faced with addressing long-deferred building infrastructure issues, The DIA took the opportunity to launch a comprehensive reinstallation project that would fundamentally change the way visitors experienced the museum. Tracking and timing studies conducted in the galleries at the onset of the project clearly showed that visitors were not engaging with the art or the text-based interpretation in numbers that satisfied the staff.[3] To remain viable, the DIA could no longer continue to engage in outputs that met only the interests of the art historical field and its connoisseurs. Museum leadership refocused the reinstallation on the DIA visitor experience by asking multidisciplinary staff teams to recreate the galleries based on what they knew about the collections *and* extensive visitor research and evaluation. All decisions about the galleries — object selection, the stories that would be told, and the interpretive strategies used — were to be measured against seven visitor-centered outcomes agreed upon by the teams. The outcomes ranged from "Visitors will feel welcome and comfortable throughout their visit" to "Visitors will form deeper, more intimate relationships with works of art by deepening their skills of looking and interpretation."[4]

On the cusp of launching its major architectural expansion, the AGO delved into a strategic planning process that included drafting institutional values. The key value that emerged: "the visitor experience is paramount." The articulation and focus on this value launched a complete rethinking of how this institution would plan and install its new galleries. A multidisciplinary team (including interpretive planners and educators) was charged with developing institutional criteria for visitor experiences in exhibitions. Early into their task the team realized that strategic planning could not move forward without first defining the overall outcomes the AGO hoped to achieve with its exhibition program. It became clear that a broader framework for planning exhibitions was needed. In response to this need, the team developed six guiding principles for AGO programming: diversity, relevance, responsiveness, creativity, transparency, and forum. The result of this process was that AGO's leadership recognized that engaging its public in compelling and innovative experiences with art should be the foundation of all their efforts. In order for the AGO to be successful in the future, its programming

must reflect diverse art, audiences, and experiences; be relevant and responsive to our communities; inspire individual creativity; contribute to institutional transparency; and provide a forum for active dialogue about art,
ideas, and related issues.

While art museums were realizing the precarious nature of their relationship with their publics and connecting it to their forecasts for future
visitation and revenue, education departments continued to focus efforts on
engaging visitors and facilitating personal meaning-making in the galleries.
At the DIA, staff with the new title "interpretive educator" had begun col-
laborating with curators on early planning for special exhibitions. The education department was also developing an in-house evaluation and visitor
research program. An educator who had been working on technology projects
was charged with working exclusively on visitor research and evaluation for
the department; an assistant was hired soon after.[5] The aesthetic development theories of Abigail Housen were deepening DIA educators' understanding of how visitors were approaching art on a cognitive level.[6] Sound
pedagogy and knowledge of how people learn grounded this new work. Significantly, the DIA education department expanded to include professionals
with expertise beyond art history and education and absorbed staff with
backgrounds in postcolonial, interdisciplinary, and museum studies. This
shift helped broaden the opportunities for connecting art to human experience, and encouraged staff to think about art in ways other than the traditional art historical frameworks. These education department initiatives
gave the DIA a firm foundation on which to build a new visitor-centered
museum.

The AGO realized that in order to fulfill its "visitor experience is paramount" institutional value it not only needed additional human resources,
but also to manage these resources in a new way. Interpretive planners,
formerly embedded in curatorial teams, were moved to the Education Department, positioning them within a team of like-minded colleagues. Importantly, the new position of Assistant Director of Education was created to
help manage the department's growing responsibilities related to institution's ongoing movement towards prioritizing the visitor. This position was
filled by an individual with expertise in the areas that were, and still are, becoming new institutional priorities for the AGO: interpretation and visitor
research.

During comprehensive reinstallation and building projects at the AGO
and the DIA, the influence of staff in the education department increased

dramatically as both museums committed to making visitor experiences more relevant and meaningful. Educators were instrumental in determining new exhibition planning processes, developing new text standards, and shaping visitor outcomes and guiding principles. Both the AGO and DIA planned gallery spaces dedicated to visitor interaction, discussion, and feedback. With curatorial partners, educators developed concepts, themes, and issues to help guide the selection and placement of art in order to best facilitate visitor engagement.

By leading the development of all interpretive strategies, including the writing of gallery text, education staff at both museums helped to bring a new matrix of planning considerations to the table. This included factoring in varied ways of learning, different motivations for visiting, and the inclusion of multiple voices and perspectives. The resulting texts, audio, video, and feedback and art-making stations are meant to stimulate conversation while engaging visitors' imaginations, creativity, ideas, and emotions. They eschew the concept of a singular "right" way to understand artworks. The privileged position of an authoritative museum voice is being replaced by multiple voices acknowledging multiple meanings.

FROM MARGIN TO CENTER?

In order to discuss the future of museum educators in interpretation, it is important to consider the traditional place of educators in museums, and why they are so well-positioned to advocate for real change in how visitors connect with art in the galleries. Educators have traditionally played only a supporting role, if any, in institutional and exhibition planning at senior levels. As Graeme Talboys explains, education was "often regarded by other members of that community as being not quite a true museum job."[7] Since museum educators devote most of their time to thinking about the public, their work has often existed apart from the focus of many museums: their art collections. This can "lead to a situation in which many museum educators are constitutionally and psychologically isolated from the mainstream of museum."[8] (Although many are art historians by training, art museum educators have been distanced from direct work with the collections. Instead, their work was often conceived in reaction to the decisions of others. Educators translated content provided by curators into training sessions for public tours and packages for teachers, and created engaging programs for children, ancillary lectures and other programs in spaces separated from the galleries. While this is important work that requires great skill and experience, it had no impact on the conceptualization or implementation of the museum's traditional programming and financial focus: the exhibition of art.

There is no doubt that space is political, both figuratively and literally. One experiences this phenomenon physically in many museums. Galleries devoted to public programming and education, as well as educators' offices, are often located in basements of multi-storied museums; activities created by education departments have traditionally been relegated to small side or end rooms in exhibitions instead of being fully integrated throughout the exhibition experience. As professionals long challenged by locative politics, using interpretation to help carve out space for visitors and their personal meaning-making is not much of a professional stretch for many educators.

As educators at museums such as AGO and DIA become more instrumental in defining visitor experiences, some in the greater art museum education field seek to position this shift as educators moving from the periphery to the center of pre-established hierarchal modes of operation.[9] This initially sounds very appealing. The opportunity to move to the top of the food chain is something for which we all, almost instinctually, yearn. But in heralding a new era for educators, do we risk ignoring the potential power of the margins?

Through the lens of the politics of location, finding a space in which to locate the work of change in museums becomes important. Margins are often considered to be sites of disconnection and deprivation: however, black feminist theorist bell hooks also writes about them as places of radical possibilities.[10] Indeed, according to hooks, the margin is the very place from which to challenge dominance and deconstruct hierarchical power.[11] This way of thinking from hooks inspires us to question the language and therefore the very nature of change in art museums: if art museum educators are indeed moving from margin to center, do they risk losing the holistic perspective that enriches their visitor-focused work?

Following hooks' polemic, as inhabitants of museums' margins, educators are in fact better positioned to be agents of the museum's transformation from lone voice of authority to social conversant. Thinking of the margins as a site of resistance, we create a new location from which to articulate visitors' points of view and to accommodate a multiplicity of voices. It also helps us champion new models for museum organizational structures; models that help flatten the hierarchy to make room for new perspectives — including the visitors—at the senior management and strategic planning levels.

Operating from the margins has distinct advantages, the foremost being point of view. As hooks explains, "To be in the margin is to be part of the whole but outside the main body."[12] A peripheral position means developing a particular way of seeing reality, that is to say, developing an understanding of the operations of both margin and the center, not only the center.[13] The result is a holistic point of view of the entire structure. This metaphor is entirely applicable to museum educators. They must be experts in not only education, but also have knowledge of museology, communications, pedagogy, and, yes, collections. At the same time, curators—the collections specialists traditionally operating at the center—until very recently have not been well-versed in museum-related fields outside of their specialty.[14] Suddenly, operating at the center does not seem as appealing as the periphery.

hooks describes margins as sites of openness, possibility, creativity and transformation. Does not this also describe the kinds of experiences many art museums are now striving to facilitate in their galleries? And does not it also describe the kinds of organizational structures we would like to work within?

As good as it may sound, declaring that educators are becoming central figures in museums is problematic. Firstly because, in many instances, this simply is not the case. While there are individual museums that have taken significant steps in this direction, discussion of the visitors' personal meaning making, accessible (as opposed to academic) exhibition texts, and the inclusion of interpretive strategies in spaces where art is installed are simply not options at many institutions. Secondly, as discussed above, margins have something to offer those who inhabit them. The educator's particular way of seeing from both the margins and the center and the multiplicity of voices that this implies, imparts educators with the kind of knowledge and skill required to lead the movement towards creating spaces and organizational structures that inspire truly dynamic, inclusive and relevant visitor experiences with art.

For both the AGO and DIA, the change from focusing solely on the art historical content of their collections to planning for dynamic visitor experiences has meant that the positions of their respective education departments are indeed shifting. After years of knocking on the door, trying with little success to participate in meaningful conversations about the larger institutional issues, interpretive staff in education departments at some art institutions now hear frequent knocks on their own doors. Educators are becoming more valued within these institutions for their expertise in how visitors learn, interpretive strategies that facilitate meaning-making, visitor research and feedback gathering, teamwork and collaboration, and success measurement tools. Educators are redefining their relationships with curators, designers, editors, and senior management while becoming leaders and drivers of significant internal processes. They are working towards the creation of museum spaces that resemble the kind of margins about which hooks writes: spaces of openness, possibility, creativity, and transformation.

If educators wish to continue fostering meaningful connections with visitors while gradually becoming more involved in museums' operational centers, they need to keep their office doors open to the center and their windows open to the margin. As the center continues to reshape itself with increased input from educators and the public, the margins also change. As the place where multiple viewpoints live, the margins are never static, with new voices and opportunities continually emerging. By remaining accessible and open to the margins — a world of possibility and transformation — we can maintain the holistic viewpoint that is so important to all that we do. In this way, when we are asked if the ideological home of education departments has moved from margin to center, we can say, thankfully not.

Notes

1. bell hooks does not capitalize her name.
2. Institute of Arts reopened to the public in November 2007, with all galleries (approximately 130) completely reinstalled and reinterpreted. The Art Gallery of Ontario's transformed building will reopen in November 2008, with almost fifty percent more exhibition space and 110 reinstalled galleries.
3. Information is from an unpublished DIA tracking and timing report written by Ken Morris and Matt Sikora in 2004.
4. Many of the DIA's key reinstallation documents, including a full list of visitor outcomes, will be published in 2009 and available at www.dia.org.
5. The DIA's investment in evaluation and visitor study was strengthened recently when Matt Sikora and Ken Morris formed the new DIA evaluation department. Separate from the education department, they now work with a broader range of museum divisions, including the senior leadership team.
6. An early document studied by DIA staff was Hausen's *Validating a Measure of Aesthetic Development for Museums and Schools*, published in the ILVS Review in 1992. Throughout the 1990s and following, all professional staff attended Visual Thinking Strategies workshops, not only as training for tours, but to better understand how visitors approach the viewing of art.
7. Graeme Talboys, The Museum Educator's Handbook, (Aldershot, UK: Ashgate Publishing Co., 2005), 19.
8. Ibid.

9. For example, *From Periphery to Center: Art Museum Education in the 21st Century*, ed by Pat Villeneuve.

10. bell hooks's work is based on issues of race and gender in society. Though we find her theory a useful way to consider the power dynamics within museum organizational structures, we do not mean to suggest that the disconnection she discusses with regard to black people in society is equal to the situation faced by the largely white, middle class women of the museum education field. However, her writings provide inspiration for all of those in marginalized situations and using the lens she provides helps us explore this situation in a new way.

11 bell hooks, Yearning: Race, Gender, and Cultural Politics (Cambridge, MA: South End Press,1990), 151.

12. Ibid, 149.

13. Ibid.

14. Lisa C. Roberts, From Knowledge to Narrative: Educators and the Changing Museum (Washington, DC: Smithsonian, 1997), ? .

References

hooks, bell. Yearning: Race, Gender, and Cultural Politics. Cambridge, MA: South End Press, 1990.

Roberts, Lisa C. From Knowledge to Narrative: Educators and the Changing Museum. Washington, DC: Smithsonian, 1997.

Talboys, Graeme. The Museum Educator's Handbook. Aldershot, UK: Ashgate Publishing Co., 2005.

Jennifer Wild Czajkowski is the Director of Interpretive Programs at the Detroit Institute of Arts. In 1997, she was hired to build an interpretive work group within the DIA's education department. She led the interpretive team for the museum's recent comprehensive reinstallation project.

Shiralee Hudson Hill is an interpretive planner at the Art Gallery of Ontario in Toronto. Prior to joining the AGO, she was a consultant with the international museum planning firm Lord Cultural Resources and has also held positions with the National Museum of Ireland in Dublin and the Ontario Science Centre in Toronto.

How a Museum Discovered
the Transforming Power of Play

Scott G. Eberle

Abstract   In 2006 the Strong Museum in Rochester, New York reopened as the Strong National Museum of Play. Devising a new interpretive plan proved crucial to transforming the institution's mission and
decisive in leading toward a $37 million expansion that drove strong
gains in attendance. Still, the new interpretive direction, articulated in
the museum's internal interpretive document, *A Framework for Interpreting
Play*, first drafted in 2002, was but one of the steps among many along
the way toward the institution's re-birth.

The search for an institutional identity actually stretched back thirty years,
all the way to the museum's founding. Chief among them was the widely
shared opinion among board and staff that the institution had not yet
reached its potential to attract local and regional audiences. Certainly some
of the forces that conspired to marginalize nearly all American museums had
born down on the Strong Museum. For example, shopping malls competed
for potential visitors' time, and television watching and video-game playing
tended to keep people at home. In the years just before this major expansion,
museum attendance plateaued at an average of about 350,000 guests annually. The figure was respectable at about five times greater than the low
point of near to 70,000 twenty years earlier. But the board and its senior leadership were not satisfied to let attendance gains stall.

From the beginning managing and interpreting a large, assorted collection had topped the list of internal challenges facing the institution.
Margaret Woodbury Strong, the largest individual holder of Eastman Kodak
stock, left an estate of $80 million in 1969. She left an enormous number of
things behind as well. Strong had collected grandly during the 1960s, and

she had delighted in leading small groups through the large home that she called her "Museum of Fascinations." Among the most fascinating things she showed her visitors were toys and dolls; hers was believed to be the largest and most comprehensive privately held collection in the world. Other collections filled every available niche in the house: furniture and household appliances, paintings and drawings, clothing, coins and stamps, Asian art, handicrafts, and decorative knickknacks by the tens of thousands. The assemblage was impressive for its size and variety, and a board organized to administer her will reserved the largest share of her estate to support a museum that would hold these things. The Margaret Woodbury Strong Museum opened in 1982 to showcase a collection of nearly half a million objects that its benefactor had gathered.

The museum's short, interesting history quickly brought a second order question—the interpretive challenge—to the fore. It was not at all clear what this vast assemblage meant, what interpretive purpose it could serve, or what audiences it would attract. Unlike the circumstances of those cabinets of curiosities that formed in an era before professional museum management, a professional staff interrogated Margaret Woodbury Strong's collections to discover their interpretive potential. In 1973, the first director, Holman J. Swinney, invited experts from Colonial Williamsburg, the New York Historical Association, Old Sturbridge Village, the Parke-Bernet Galleries, the Smithsonian Institution, and Winterthur to assess the collection. The consultants faced a large and somewhat daunting task. Their consensus proved as interesting for the options passed up as for the choices recommended and followed. Those consultants confirmed the strength of the doll and toy collection and saw that "children," "play," "imagination," and "fun" could become fruitful interpretive themes. But speaking for the rest of the group, one of the consultants conceded to "an instinctive…mental, cultural, and perhaps even a 'moral' block against…dolls…paintings, tin toys" and the rest.

The group discovered, however, that they could posit the interpretive message amidst the variety and assumed triviality of the collection. Because, they observed, most of the museum's objects shared an origin in the late nineteenth and early twentieth centuries and because most were the product of mass manufacturing, the group deduced that the museum should instead interpret America's products and the means of producing them during America's industrializing period between 1820 and 1940. Here was a meat and potatoes approach connecting the collections with epochal changes of the American past. And so the museum debuted in its new space in 1982 with exhibits about America's transition from rural life to a modernizing industrial economy, the ideology of middle-class home life, and furniture design. Accordingly, exhibitions about flow-blue china, childhood collecting, gardening, dining, kerosene lighting, rustic furniture, and other aspects of domestic life followed. Noteworthy exhibits such as *The Great Transformation* (1982), *Fit for America: Health, Fitness, Sport and American Society, 1830-1940* (1986), and *Culture and Comfort: People, Parlors, and Upholstery, 1850-1930* (1988) illustrated the modernization hypothesis and trends in material culture study. The museum also devoted twenty-thousand square feet of glass cases to un-interpreted "study collections" numbering about 18,000 artifacts for the instruction of connoisseurs. Such open access to collections was almost unprecedented and represented a laudable transparency ordinarily missing in museums.

In the first year after opening, the museum entertained 150,000 curiosity-seekers, but conveying the interpretive mission to a popular audience proved challenging. Un-interpreted collections fared even less well because audiences with a progressively smaller store of personal recollection found the things harder to explain. Emotional associations also cooled with time. With each passing year memories of grandma's hurricane lamp faded to second-hand knowledge; artifacts that had formerly "spoken" eloquently began to fall silent. A display of hundreds of disembodied doll heads in the study collections proved to be a bonanza to those few who were interested in historical materials, but more often casual visitors found the sight of them slightly unsettling. Unhappily too, because recondite interpretation in exhibits appealed to few, within three years local visitors had largely satisfied their curiosity. Attendance fell to fewer than 70,000 by 1985 and threatened to fall farther after most had been there and done that. Plainly it was not enough that a major museum should collect and preserve things and inform its audiences; survival depended upon charming them, too.

Finding that attractive spot where appeal met education became the work of the next decade. It would not be sufficient to respond by changing exhibits' tone; it became clearer over time that if the museum hoped to avoid irrelevance the very nature of the institution needed changing. The museum targeted a broader audience with *One History Place* (1987), a hands-on recreated Victorian parlor for children seven and younger that gave them (and their parents) a feel for the era's overstuffed chairs, fussy tea sets and fancy clothes, hand-laundering, scratch recipes, and do it yourself entertainment.

In this space young children played to learn and adults learned from their play. This proved a winning pedagogy.

Because of its success, *One History Place* also succeeded for a time in helping the museum overlook the tension growing between the two main but mismatched interpretive approaches—an interest in the decorative arts and an interest in interpreting social history from the bottom up (an approach widely heralded as the *new* social history). The first arose in an aesthetic preoccupation that attended to design and display in the late-nineteenth century middle class home. One of the original consultants of the 1970s, Richard Grove, a Deputy Assistant Secretary for History at the Smithsonian, had noted that the collections and the history of popular taste that they could support had a "feminine bias" in this focus on domestic life and "women's sphere." The second drew strength from the history of the working class, the history of the factory, and the history of labor—largely male territory that the institution would never seriously expect to document. The clever structure the consultants had erected exposed cracks that ran along gender lines.

Even if the two had been able to travel comfortably, neither approach could have much helped raise the museum's community profile. However, in the early 90s, the museum determined to join current community discussions with exhibits that highlighted issues such as advertising, bereavement, the rise of the middle class, life on the wartime home-front, alcohol and drug use, racism, environmental history, and health care. The drive toward relevance in interpretation coincided with a thoroughgoing re-orientation of management processes toward "customer service." In a word, with its appetite for change sharpened both in its interpretation and in its way of doing business, the museum would become more responsive.

Two key changes in basic interpretation had helped this process along: eliminating the "end-date" of 1940 that had prevented exhibits from addressing current concerns, and refocusing interpretation on issues related to the cultural history of progress, identity, and class. This was a fertile, demanding period for exhibit development. Exhibits such as *Memory and Mourning: American Expressions of Grief* (1993), *Between 2 Worlds: African-American Identity and American Culture* (1994), and *Say Ahh! Examining America's Health* (1995) enlisted community advisory groups to help shape interpretation. Media coverage rose appreciably as the museum reestablished local contact. Attendance roughly doubled. But attendance would not jump again until a series of exhibits that began with *When Barbie Dated G.I. Joe: America's*

Romance with Cold War Toys (1994), *Small Wonders: A Fantastic Voyage into the Miniature World* (1995), and *Kid to Kid* (1996) culminated with *Super Kids Market* and *Can You Tell Me How to Get to Sesame Street?*, (both 1997). A long experiment in education and entertainment had finally made room at the museum for Big Bird and a new emphasis on contemporary culture.

The success of playful and highly interactive exhibits such as *Timelab* (1999), *Toys from Mars* (2001), and *Making Radio Waves* (2002) helped direct interpretation back to the option that the initial team of experts could not bring themselves to recommend. One question began to pop up periodically: could play itself join progress, identity, and class as a guiding interpretive light? Could play finally enable the museum to capitalize intellectually and programmatically on the true core of its collections—all those dolls, toys, and other artifacts of play? The question was slightly awkward; after all, wasn't play and its rich associations in cultural history, evolutionary psychology, and educational methodology more like a mission in itself? But the basic challenge remained—finding a way to pursue the mission and interpret the collection so that medium and message and subject and object could coincide. Exhibit experience, educational approaches, the collections' manifest strengths, and new geo-demographic surveys conducted in 2002 encouraged staff to think that this was possible. But the institution still stood a distance off from bringing play to the center of interpretation. One hurdle delayed a journey back to the future, namely the same tendency to confuse gravity with profundity that restrained the original examiners: if it was fun, it couldn't be important.

It may have seemed to some that *A Framework for Interpreting Play*, written without outside consultation in the first few weeks of 2002, had sprung full grown from the creative foam. But, in fact, much had come to pass in the intervening three decades to change the opinion that had once weighed in so heavily against play. Four factors, two external and two internal proved most relevant.

1. Successful children's museums had sprouted around the country, proving the audience appeal of play.
2. Play scholarship had blossomed in disciplines such as history, anthropology, developmental and educational psychology, psychiatry, philosophy, and neuroscience, and this gave the subject new depth and gravity.
3. Play had never been completely submerged at the museum. Over the years a number of smaller temporary exhibits such as *Yesterday's Play-*

things (1982), *Golf in Rochester* (1989), and *Handcrafts and Hobbies* (1991) had kept a small votive flame burning for play.
4. And, of course, the museum's premiere collections, its main assets, had always needed friendly integration and unapologetic interpretation.

In the late 1980s, the museum made a commitment to systematic strategic planning that board and staff would update annually. Strategic planning proved crucial as it drove a deliberate, evolutionary process of discovering the institution's identity. Planning entailed joint board-staff benchmarking trips to other museums in the mid-1990s followed by audience surveys and zip code by zip code profiling of the regional market. By the turn of the 21st century both external and internal pressures encouraged ambitions for systematic change. Early in 2003 the museum's Executive Committee deputized a Board-Staff Play Study Team to consider the pros and cons of bringing play to the center of museum activities. The team was charged with exploring such basic questions as finding a workable definition of play and projecting the themes and exhibits that definition would support; forecasting the impact on educational programs, membership, and attendance; answering whether or not the museum would need to change its mission statement; assessing the impact of a mission change on marketing, financing, fundraising, and human resources; and projecting the effects of the stimulus of new collecting. Answering these broad-ranging questions about changing the institution's mission linked the museum's most important fiduciary, civic, and intellectual responsibilities. And so, when in 2004 the museum's board voted to adopt a new mission to explore play "in order to encourage learning, creativity, and discovery," it seemed more like a homecoming than a wondrous birth.

In 2006, new attractions of the expanded museum included the *Dancing Wings Butterfly Garden*, the 12,000 square foot *Reading Adventureland*—an interactive history of children's literature, and space for the Woodbury Preschool, which engages its pupils in a play curriculum. The museum's signature exhibit *Field of Play* opened to invite guests to experience and reenact the elements of play—anticipation, surprise, pleasure, understanding, strength, and poise—in a play environment that features paired time-trial dragsters, a crooked house, a Dance Dance Revolution machine, a pretend underwater-scape, and an "Ames" room which surprises the muscles and the mind with its deceptive, off-kilter proportions. Broadly, *Field of Play* is about play as human development, play as a social phenomenon, and play as an individual experience. The exhibit demonstrates that play is basic to human nature, and that understanding play is important to understanding culture and the way culture changes.

The new mission made play the museum's main subject, but play is also literally the object. *Field of Play* connects ideas about play to real play experiences now and in the past with dozens of low and high-tech interactive elements and more than four hundred artifacts. The objects and the interpretive exhibit in which they take life make clear that dolls and toys, the core strength of the museum's collections, are not trivial because these artifacts cultivate the imagination, channel creativity, and encourage critical and strategic thinking. Toys require us to cooperate in play and so teach us fairness. They disclose what we believed and what we valued and sometimes what we dismissed or feared. Toys, in fact, are among the most revealing artifacts that humans have produced. The toys of our past, the perennial favorites, preserve the inspirations, technologies, marketing strategies, and sometimes even the ideologies of their time as they changed to meet new demand. Toys, games, models, clothing, chemistry sets, paintings, sports gear, trophies, books, t-shirts, and magic tricks, all remind us how we embrace play. Play helps us imagine what's next, and so, along the way, toys also often reveal who we hope to become.

The result? Product and process have co-evolved to deliver a remade museum. Play has become the museum's method of instruction; the message has become the medium as it invites visitors to understand the critical role of play in learning, creativity, and discovery. And the museum has moved to extend its curiosity. Volume 1, number 1 of a new scholarly periodical, the *American Journal of Play*, appeared in July, 2008 and it carries the work of historians, neuroscientists, sociologists, psychologists, physicians, anthropologists, and folklorists who study play. Museum attendance is now nearly ten times higher than it was at its nadir twenty five years before, evidence that the Strong National Museum of Play has at long last retrieved the old sense of "The Museum of Fascinations" that had driven its founder. The museum's President and CEO, G. Rollie Adams summed the new interpretive thrust this way, "Strong has circled back to its founder and core collections and has created, finally, a museum of play."

Notes

1. Adams, G. Rollie. "Board-Staff Play Study Team Notebook," Strong National Museum of Play Archives, January 9, 2003.
2. Adams, G. Rollie and Scott G. Eberle. "Making Room for Big Bird," *History News* 51, no. 4 (Autumn, 1996): 23-26.
3. Adams, G. Rollie. "Ready, Set, *Go*: Finally a Museum for Play," *History News* 61, no 3 (March, 2007): 7-11.
4. Eberle, Scott G. *A Framework for Interpreting Play* (Strong National Museum of Play Archives, 2006).
5. Eberle, Scott G.. "Memory and Mourning: An Exhibit History," *Death Studies* 29, no 6 (July/August 2005): 535-557.
6. Sandler, Carol. "Strong Museum Exhibitions," (Strong National Museum of Play Archives, 2008)
7. Weil, Stephen E. "From Being about Something to Being for Somebody: The Ongoing Transformation of the American Museum," *Daedalus* 128, no. 3 (Summer, 1999): 1, 17.
8. Long-Range Planning Committee Strong National Museum of Play, Strong National Museum of Play Archives .*Strong National Museum of Play, Strategic Plan, 2004-2009: Fourth Update.* December 4, 2007.

Scott G. Eberle Ph.D., Vice President for Interpretation at the Strong National Museum of Play since 1989, is also Senior Associate Editor for the new American Journal of Play. His works in progress include Classic Toys of the National Toy Hall of Fame *(Running Press, 2009), and forthcoming with Stuart Brown, M.D.:* The Elements of Play: An Exploration in Culture, History, and Evolutionary Neuroscience. *Eberle's next exhibit project is tentatively titled* Superheroes and the Battle for Good over Evil.

Building Balance
Integrating Interpretive Planning in a Research Institution

Jim S. H. Hakala

Abstract   Ideally, the process and product of interpretive planning is a living document that serves to guide a museum's interpretation proactively. This case study details the development and resulting benefits of the first institution-wide interpretive plan at the University of Colorado Museum of Natural History. Stimulated by internal growth and change, the institution-wide interpretive plan brought a solid sense of unity, focused direction, and a strong public message to a venerable research institution.

Established in 1902, University of Colorado Museum of Natural History (UCMNH) is an academic unit of the Graduate School at the University of Colorado in Boulder. The Museum sustains a dynamic research program, offers a wide range of special events and educational programs, and houses the Museum and Field Studies Graduate Program. With over four million specimens and artifacts, the UCMNH preserves the largest natural history collection in the Rocky Mountain region. The Museum's mission is to foster exploration and appreciation of the natural environment and human cultures through research, teaching, and community outreach.

The Museum, which is governed by the University of Colorado, operates as a department within the University and utilizes an Advisory Board of community representatives for planning and fundraising. The UCMNH is currently organizationally, and to some extent physically, divided into two sections that focus on the research or public aspects of the Museum's mission. The Museum's seven curators, who focus on anthropology, botany, entomology, palaeontology, and zoology, are tenure-track faculty at the University. The Museum's public space consists of three permanent galleries (Palaeontology, Biology, and Anthropology) as well as two changing

©2008 Museum Education Roundtable. All rights reserved.

exhibition galleries. Public and school programs are offered largely in those exhibition spaces and consist of a full complement of school, family, and adult programs.

Two sources stimulated the development of an Institutional-wide Interpretive Plan (IIP). First, the three permanent gallery spaces — each installed in different decades — were somewhat dated and insular; each spoke strongly to its collection but not to a unifying theme or to the Museum's mission. Poised to embark on a series of renovations, the staff needed to articulate the themes that would guide the reinstallation plans. Secondly, over the last number of years, the Museum's public aspects had matured and professionalized (with its first full-time program, education, and visitor services staff) and was in search of its role in the community. Additionally, in order to find its niche and a broader audience, the Museum needed to situate itself relative to its larger neighbor, the Denver Museum of Nature and Science (DMNS). The UCMNH spoke to a different message and experience, but what was that message and experience? We needed to clearly explain to a potential audience the role we played in the community and the reason it should attend our Museum. To do that, we needed to be clear in both our purpose and of what that experience would be for our visitors.

Having recently transitioned from an exhibition-led model, with education and public programs acting in a predominately responsive mode, to an integrated model of project development where exhibition, programs, education, and the web site are developed in concert, the staff honed strong collaborative and integrated planning skills. To this end, the Museum's Public Section staff held a retreat in July of 2005., The group, comprising six people, represented the Museum's exhibition, education, public programs, visitor services, and website functions.

The first step was to establish an Intellectual Framework: the underlying conceptual structure that focuses the Museum's public efforts. This Framework is built around the Museum's mission and the stakeholders' needs, and it is rooted in the Museum's research and collecting. It is the organizing principle for the ideas and themes that guide exhibits and programming and is applied to all aspects of the Public Section's work so that any visitor to the Museum leaves having heard that message generally and supporting messages specifically. In short, it is the story we, the UCMNH, want to tell.

Rather than simply telling important science stories, we feel our key message is to use those stories to demonstrate the importance of ongoing collecting and research — why the exploration and appreciation of the natural environment and human cultures matters and, ultimately, why the work of the University of Colorado matters. This message was tested against the three existing permanent galleries as well as recent temporary exhibitions and programs. It was found to have effective cross disciplinary links that could continue to reinforce a strong story line across disparate collections and exhibitions. The IIP details this key message with examples of how that story is played out in individual collections and research projects. The plan further articulates a potential five year schedule for the permanent galleries' reinstallation utilizing this framework, with the most detail outlined for the Palaeontology Hall — the first scheduled renovation — to be used as a model for future renovations.

The IIP, upon completion by the Public Section staff and acceptance by the Director, was presented to the full Museum faculty and staff for review and approval. While the faculty and staff had seen earlier drafts of the IIP, this was an important opportunity to underscore the common goal of what were organizationally two sections of the Museum. The Museum faculty and staff unanimously approved the IIP.

In the following months, the IIP had great utility in the reinstallation of the new Palaeontology Hall. It helped us establish priorities for resource allocation and visitor experiences. It was a useful tool in securing University support for the project and engaging faculty scientists in the process. Important stories about how these ancient specimens had busy contemporary lives in research and how that research helped scientists answer important questions today were told through traditional fossil exhibit elements and audio visual and computer interactives.

About a year after the original IIP was adopted, the Public Section held another retreat to revisit the IIP with a specific focus on how the identified messages would be emphasized through programs for families, adults, and school groups. The resulting complete plan unifies the UCMNH Public Section's direction and messages for all its offerings and work and works in concert with the research sections.

As time has passed and as we continue to use the IIP, three key benefits of the Institution-wide Interpretive Plan are evident:

Clarity and Strength of Direction

Research staff better understand the Public Section of the Museum as integral to their work rather than a separate Section focussed on pubic service.

The Public Section staff is confident that its programs work together to communicate clear and cohesive message and making decisions about what programs to include or support are easier.

Unity of effort

Rather than seeing individual roles as serving discrete institutional goals, individual staff — even within the Public Section — now understand their roles as part of a larger whole which contributes to a single, institutional goal rather than separate, departmental goals.

Strong Public Message

Struggling to build its attendance as well as public awareness, the Museum now has a clear message to share and reinforce across all program offerings and public communications. It has a simple and compelling message to communicate to its public that is inclusive, relevant, and contemporary.

The University of Colorado Museum of Natural History's Institution-wide Interpretive Plan is a living document that changes with time, science priorities, and society. In March of 2008, the Museum began a new era with new leadership, and, while the Museum's IIP will most likely be revisited and possibly revised, what will not change is the important clarifying and unifying role the IIP plays for the Museum.

Jim Hakala (james.hakala@colorado.edu) is the Assistant Director at the University of Colorado Museum of Natural History and currently serves as the Chair of the Executive Board of the American Association of Museum's Standing Professional Committee on Education (EdCom). Jim chaired the Task Force that developed AAM EdCom's Excellence in Practice: Museum Education Principles and Standards in 2002 (revised 2005) and has served as Board Member at Large and Vice President of the Museum Education Roundtable. Special thanks to Judy Koke for her help in preparing this article.

An Interpretive Master Plan at the Museum of Fine Arts, Houston

Beth B. Schneider

Abstract   This case study presents the methods the staff at the Museum of Fine Arts, Houston used to develop and implement an interpretive master plan from 1996-2000. The process can be a model for other museums. Looking back a decade after the plan was developed provides insights into the role of interpretive plans as statements of goals, expressions of ideals, and plans of work that can provide flexibility in guiding museums over many years.

This case study presents the methods the staff at the Museum of Fine Arts, Houston used to develop and implement an interpretive master plan from 1996-2000. The process can be a model for other museums. Looking back a decade after the plan was developed provides insights into the role of interpretive plans as statements of goals, expressions of ideals, and plans of work that can provide flexibility in guiding museums over many years.

INTRODUCTION/CONTEXT

In writing an interpretive master plan, as in developing any interpretive publications or programs, it is essential to know the museum context in which the plan will be implemented and the intended audience for the plan. In 1996 and 1997, at the Museum of Fine Arts, Houston (MFAH), the staff developed an interpretive master plan as part of the expansion of the museum which comprised constructing a new museum building, which opened in 2000, and reinstallation of the museum's entire collection of world art in the new Audrey Jones Beck Building and the existing Caroline Weiss Law Building. The MFAH identified two main audiences for the interpretive master plan. The first audience encompassed the MFAH staff in education,

Journal of Museum Education, Volume 33, Number 3, Fall 2008, pp. 277–282.

curatorial, visitor services, publications, exhibition design and beyond. A interpretive master plan was deemed essential for all involved in the massive reinstallation of the collection, the development labels, wall texts, materials for teachers and for families, and audio tours while maintaining and expanding an ambitious schedule of programs. We believed that the plan would help articulate goals and objectives and guide our work. The interpretive master plan existed alongside the MFAH's long-range plan for the entire institution, but was intended to provide a format for developing interpretive materials in the galleries and education programs and publications.

The second audience, external to the museum, comprised governmental agencies, private foundations, corporations, and individuals, all potential funders of the large capital campaign the MFAH undertook to pay for the expansion. The interpretive master plan was also a complement to a 1995 book written by MFAH staff that surveyed all existing MFAH education programs and a history of education at the institution.[1] The director Peter C. Marzio deemed this combination of history, represented by the book, and forward thinking as presented in the interpretive master plan, as essential to informing potential funders about the past and the future of the MFAH.

PRECEDENT

The MFAH[2] built on the experience in 1991-1993 of developing an interpretive plan for its Bayou Bend Collection and Gardens when the building was updated and the collection of American painting, furniture, and decorative arts dating from 1640-1880 was reinstalled. The project at Bayou Bend enabled curators and educators to work with a team of national consultants, focus the interpretive themes for the Bayou Bend Collection, and design interpretive programs and materials. The National Endowment for the Humanities (NEH) provided the funding for and proved to be an important aspect of the Bayou Bend project. NEH funding made it possible to bring in experts and also provided an important seal of approval for the entire project. The success of this project set the stage for developing an interpretive master plan for the collection of world art at the MFAH.

PROCESS

Developing the interpretive master plan involved several components. Teams of MFAH staff—educators, curators, and visitor services—visited four other museums to observe their approaches to interpretation and to meet with their educators, curators, and directors. Three art museums—the Minneapolis Institute of Arts, the Denver Art Museum, and the Indianapolis Museum of Art—were selected for their excellence in education and interpretation and their similarity in size and scope to the MFAH. The Boston Children's Museum allowed us to learn from an innovative museum in which the concerns of the audience were of paramount importance. For our museum visits, we first approached the museums as visitors, then as museum professionals with an extensive questionnaire focusing on interpretation and amenities. An unintended but incredibly important outcome of these visits was the camaraderie that grew among the MFAH staff teams through the shared experiences that served as a touchstone for future discussions.

Twelve outside consultants including museum directors, education directors, academics, and representatives of local schools and universities,[3] visited the MFAH individually to study the museum's exhibitions and installations, returning for a three-day meeting to exchange ideas and develop recommendations. Recommendations were divided into three categories—orientation, interpretation, and the building. The consultants unanimously agreed that people should have fun at a museum. In order to enjoy the museum, visitors must be able to find their way around easily and interact with friendly and knowledgeable museum staff and volunteers. Labels, programs, installations, and other interpretive strategies must be flexible enough to allow for changes as we learn about our audiences, and testing and evaluation should be built into all aspects of orientation and interpretation.

The great challenge of this project was balancing the desire to create an aesthetic, contemplative mood in the galleries, the need for information about works of art without overwhelming visitors, and the importance of creating a comfortable environment for visitors. Consultant David Carr noted that visitors should be "the authors of their own museum experience," exploring the MFAH on their own, choosing what to learn about, and learning in their own ways. He encouraged us to avoid any suggestion of a curriculum that must be mastered in order for visitors to have a successful museum experience. Carr noted that no visitor should feel as though s/he can "flunk the museum."

THE PLAN

Many staff members including educators, curators, visitor services staff, editors, graphic designers, exhibition designers, and museum administrators

contributed to the final form of the plan, which was drafted by the MFAH
education director as manager for the interpretive master plan project. The
MFAH plan has two sections.

> *Orientation* addresses the sprawling museum campus and focuses on
> five activities: identifying the museum's audience; inviting them into
> the museum; greeting visitors and providing them with information
> about the institution; providing directions to the museum's many fa-
> cilities; and encouraging visitors to repeat visits and to invite visitor re-
> sponses about their museum experiences.

> *Interpretation* applies to the museum's entire collection of world art to
> be installed in the Beck and Law buildings on the main campus. To
> help us come to grips with such a diverse collection, the NEH con-
> sultants recommended a set of questions to guide interpretation. They
> were: What is this? Why was it made? How was it used? How was it
> made? Who made it? How does it become art? How is it chosen or col-
> lected? Why is it in this museum? What does it mean today? Why are
> these works of art displayed together? How do I look at this?

Interpretation focused on providing visitors with many points of entry
to look at, think about, learn about, find meaning in, and enjoy the works of
art at the MFAH. This plan assumes that the museum's visitors are intel-
ligent, curious about art, and interested in learning whether they are art
museum novices or experts. The plan lists the entire range of interpretation
and programs envisioned in 1997: labels, wall texts, resources for educators,
random-access recorded tours, a web site, on-line chat groups, small focus
exhibitions, interactive spaces, hands-on materials, programs both at the
museum and off-site that comprise conversations, lectures, art-making,
writing about art, performances that link performing arts and literature to
the visual arts, and exhibitions for audiences of adults, educators, families,
and students.

IMPLEMENTING THE PLAN

As the work on the collection installation and interpretation developed from
1997-2000, five interpretive projects became priorities for completion in time
for the opening of the Beck Building in 2000. Educators and curators developed new wall texts and chat labels for hundreds of works in the MFAH
collection. A random-access audio tour in English and in Spanish provided

commentary on more than 300 works of art and brought in a wide range of voices and points of view in that interpretation. Staff worked with local artists to create hands-on materials that could be used by volunteers in the galleries to explain key techniques such as oil painting, egg tempera painting, and ceramics. A team of educators developed close to 100 Art Cards, resources for teachers on works of art in the collection. Educators and the curator of European decorative arts also developed a pilot, interpretive exhibition focusing silver in 18th century Britain.

CONCLUSION — LOOKING BACK

In fact, our plan was overly ambitious in what it attempted to accomplish in the three years of reinstallation. But it provided a blueprint for interpretive programs and materials that has guided the MFAH and the education department over the past decade. When I left the MFAH in July 2007, and looked back over the decade after the plan was developed, it was clear that many of ideas in the plan were realized, just over a longer period of time than had been originally anticipated. The MFAH redesigned its website in 2002, and, over the next six years, educators developed on-line materials for teachers, put the entire catalogue of the MFAH teacher resource center on line, and developed on-line tour booking. The MFAH only experimented with one small focus exhibition in the galleries, but in 2006-2007 the department developed interactive spaces for temporary exhibitions that provided models that could be adapted to collection galleries in the future. Funding was secured in 2007 to develop materials for families. With over 20 exhibitions a year, it was difficult to find a way to incorporate formative evaluation into exhibition didactics. But with plans for a new building in the next decade, the museum now has more experience with summative evaluation focusing on visitor learning which can be used as a basis for formative studies in the future.

I have come to see interpretive plans as both a menu of all of our best ideas and as goals to achieve in an ideal world. All of our on-going work provides a kind of research into audiences and their interactions with art and provides a basis for new ideas and approaches. The MFAH is now reinstalling its Asian galleries and the education department is working with curators on the display and interpretation of objects as an (almost) equal partner with the curators — something that is new for the institution. We never arrive at the perfect interpretive and programmatic mix because interpretation changes, ideas about art change, we learn from our experiences, and change ideas and direction. The value of these plans lies in their flexibility, encompassing both ideals and reality, working across the museum as a team, and working within the reality of our institutions.

Notes

1. *Education in the Arts: The Museum of Fine Arts, Houston.* Beth B. Schneider with Daniel J. Gorski, Joseph P. Havel and Norma R. Ory. (Houston, The Museum of Fine Arts, Houston, 1995).
2. The Museum of Fine Arts, Houston comprises a main campus with the Audrey Jones Beck and Caroline Wiess Law buildings for displaying art, a sculpture garden, an art school building, an administrative building/junior school, and a parking garage. A third building is planned for this location in the future. Two house museums, Bayou Bend for American decorative arts and Rienzi for European decorative arts, are located ten minutes from the main museum campus as is an off-site art storage and conservation facility.
3. David Carr, John Chiaravalloti, Mihaly Csikszentmihalyi, Michael Dula, David Henry, Evan Maurer, Anita Najar, Robert Patten, Patricia Steuert, Bret Waller, and Patterson Williams.

Beth B. Schneider served as Education Director at the Museum of Fine Arts, Houston from 1986 through 2007 when she was named Education Director Emeritus. From 2005 to 2007 she was the Museum Education Division Director of the National Art Education Association. Currently, Beth is Head of Education at the Royal Academy of Arts in London. Her email address is beth.schneider@royalacademy.org.uk.

An Evaluation of the Effectiveness of National Park Service Interpretive Planning

Marcella Wells

Abstract   In 2005-2006, the National Park Service Office of Interpretive Planning at Harpers Ferry Center, in collaboration with the author, conducted an evaluation project to (a) assess the appropriateness and quality of specific elements of National Park Service (NPS) interpretive plans, (b) determine where improvements in planning might be made, and (c) support the continued improvement of interpretive planning services within the agency. This article describes the process of evaluating a set of Long Range Interpretive Plans developed by the National Park Service. Based on the results of the evaluation, the article concludes with a set of refined interpretive planning principles proposed by the author.

Simply put, interpretive planning is the process by which planners (e.g., educators, interpreters, managers, and administrators) determine the most appropriate interpretive or educational prescriptions for their sites and situations. Like other types of planning, the interpretive planning should not only be a logical, rational, deliberate, and transparent process, but most importantly, should be an effort that is useful for making decisions about and implementing interpretive initiatives.

NATIONAL PARK SERVICE INTERPRETIVE PLANNING

The stimulus for this research was the 1996 circulation of an internal guideline (NPS 6 Chapter III — New Interpretation and Visitor Service Guidelines for Interpretive Planning) which addressed the reformulation of some Park Service Interpretive Master Plans. The Guideline defines interpretive planning as,

Journal of Museum Education, Volume 33, Number 3, Fall 2008, pp. 283–292.

Figure 1   Basic principles for NPS interpretive planning (NPS-6, Chapter III, 5-6):

- The interpretive planning process is goal-driven
- Interpretive plans describe visitor experience which are directed to a variety of publics, both in-park and outreach audiences
- Interpretive planning recommends appropriate interpretive services, facilities, and programs to communicate in the most effective way the park's purpose, significance, compelling stories, themes and values, while protecting and preserving park resources
- Interpretive planning will be facilitated by a person who has demonstrated competencies in interpretive planning.
- Interpretive planning is flexible, ongoing, interdisciplinary, responds to client needs and is management-oriented, rather than development or issue-driven.
- The interpretive planning process extends beyond park boundaries.
- Interpretive planning is based on current research
- Interpretive planning recommends the most current and appropriate techniques and media, suggests effective approaches for personal services, and draws upon current educational philosophy in program planning.
- Interpretive planning includes practical strategies for implementation including funding and management alternatives.

a strategic process which, in its implementation, achieves management objectives through interpretation and education....it is a goal-driven process which describes visitor experiences and recommends appropriate means to achieve them while protecting and preserving the park resources[1]

The document suggests that interpretive planning is a vital component of broader park planning and management and that NPS interpretive planning should adhere to a set of basic principles (see Figure 1, above).

The Guideline defines a Comprehensive Interpretive Plan as a collection of various planning documents and databases a park might develop over time. These include:

- a *long-range interpretive plan* (LRIP) that provides vision for the future of that park's interpretation (that might have a planning horizon of seven to ten years);
- an *annual interpretive plan* that provides interpretive direction for one year, and
- various other *reports, plans, inventories, and/or databases* gathered in one place to help facilitate the interpretive planning effort (e.g., visitor survey

data; media inventories, plans and/or evaluations; annual program reports).

INTERPRETIVE PLANNING EVALUATION

The focus of this project was on evaluating the effectiveness of Long Range Interpretive Plans (LRIP). As the first and only evaluation study of its kind to date, the hope was that results of this evaluation might render important and useful information about how to improve the efficiency, effectiveness, and utility of interpretive planning for the National Parks specifically but also of interpretive planning at-large.

Methodology

A purposive sample[2] of fourteen plans was evaluated. These plans, all written within the most recent five years of the research, were selected to represent a variety of natural and cultural areas, large and small parks, as well as urban and rural (or more remote) parks. As described in the NPS-6, Chapter III Guidelines, the plans were developed by a team that would have included Park staff, regional office staff, Harper's Ferry staff, designers and developers, media specialists, partners, and/or subject matter experts.

Based on guidance provided in NPS-6 Chapter III, an evaluation survey was developed to evaluate the effectiveness of specific plan elements — such as planning foundation, existing conditions, audience description, recommendations, implementation detail — and plan characteristics — such as, readability, appearance, usefulness. Each plan was reviewed by two separate reviewers using the survey. Reviewers included interpretive specialists and planners, chiefs of interpretation, media specialists, superintendents, and/or staff curators. All reviewers were NPS employees, but none of the reviewers had any involvement in the planning process for the Park plan s/he reviewed.

A five-point semantic differential scale (ranging from 1 = poor to 5 = excellent) was used on the reviewer survey for evaluating the various elements and characteristics of each plan (see Figure 2). In addition, reviewers were encouraged to explain, in narrative, the rationale for their scale choices and to respond to open-ended questions about the strengths of the plan and make suggestions for improvement.

Figure 2   Scale Example and Plan Variables Evaluated by Reviewers

A five-point scale such as the one below was used to by reviewers to evaluate each of the following plan elements and characteristics. In addition, reviewers were encouraged to explain their scale selection.

How would you rate the recommendations for personal interpretive services (contained in this plan)?

Poor   1_____2_____3_____4_____5   Excellent
Explain:

The following plan elements and characteristics were assessed by reviewers using the Survey form and in follow-up phone interviews.

Planning Foundation (adequacy of each element in the plan)
- Park Purpose
- Park Significance
- Primary Interpretive Themes
- Visitor Experience Goals and/or Visitor Experience Statement
- Other Foundational Elements (e.g., vision or mission statements, management goals, issues or influence affecting interpretation, related planning efforts, other background information)

Existing Conditions (rating the description of)

Audience Description (rating the description of)

Appropriateness of Recommendations (Overall, how well recommendations correspond to foundation elements)

Goals and Recommendations for Specific Services and Media
- Personal Services – goals and recommendations (evaluated separately)
- Formal Education Services – goals and recommendations (evaluated separately)
- Interpretive Media – goals and recommendations (evaluated separately)
- Interpretive Facilities – goals and recommendations (evaluated separately)

Visitor Experience(s) – (evaluation of the guidance provided in the plan for)

Overall Level of Detail

Readability

Appearance (graphics and overall design/presentation)

Perceived usefulness (of overall plan – scale ranged from Not Very to Extremely Useful)

After each plan was evaluated using the survey form, each reviewer completed a phone interview with one of two Park Service planners (coordinators of this project) to discuss the evaluations. Summaries of the phone interviews were sent to the reviewers for verification. Any confusing statements or misleading information was clarified in the final transcripts.

Findings

The evaluation rendered both quantitative and qualitative results. Table 1 displays quantitative scores for plan elements and characteristics. Qualitative results are summarized at the end of this section.

Table 1 displays mean scores across all plans for the various plan elements and characteristics evaluated in this project. On average, the strongest elements of the Park Service plans included the description of *park purpose* (4.1), *park significance* (4.3), *primary or overall themes* (4.1), *readability* (3.8), *visitor*

Table 1 Summary of Plan Element and Characteristic Mean Scores Across All Plans (n=14 plans)

Planning Foundation Elements	Mean Score (range) across all Plans	
Park Purpose	4.1 (1.0 to 5.0)	
Park Significance	4.3 (2.0 to 5.0)	
Primary/Overall Interpretive Themes	4.1 (2.0 to 5.0)	
Visitor Experience Goals/Statement	3.7 (1.0 to 5.0)	
Other Foundational Elements	3.7 (1.0 to 5.0)	
Existing Conditions	3.3 (.5 to 5.0)	
Audience Description	3.1 (1.0 to 5.0)	
Appropriateness of Recommendations	3.5 (1.5 to 5.0)	
Specific Media and Services	**Goals**	**Recommendations**
Personal Services	3.1 (1.0 to 5.0)	3.3 (1.0 to 5.0)
Formal Education Services	2.9 (1.0 to 5.0)	3.2 (1.0 to 5.0)
Interpretive Media	3.1 (1.0 to 5.0)	3.2 (1.0 to 5.0)
Interpretive Facility	3.1 (1.0 to 5.0)	3.4 (1.0 to 5.0)
Visitor Experience	3.2 (1.0 to 5.0)	
Readability	3.8 (1.0 to 5.0)	
Appearance	3.4 (1.0 to 5.0)	
Overall usefulness	3.3 (1.0 to 5.0)	

Reviewers evaluated the "adequacy" of each plan element using a 5-point scale that ranged from 1 = Poor to 5 = Excellent (see Figure 2).

experience goals (3.7), and *other foundational elements* (3.7). Elements that received lower scores included *visitor experiences* (3.2), *audience description* (3.1), and *goals* (and some *recommendations*) for the various *interpretive media and services* (2.9 to 3.2). Remaining elements received average scores (3.3 to 3.6).

Researchers[3] also content analyzed the open-ended survey results and discussion comment made during the interviews. The following comments represent the strongest (or best) elements of the plans, listed in order from most to least number of reviewer comments.

- Foundational statements (purpose, significance, themes) are strong, well-written, thorough, good
- Recommendations are consistent with foundational elements
- Goals tied to park mission; good linkages between goals and recommendations
- Specific, clear, sufficient detail
- Plan(s) is(are) readable
- Interpretive themes were good, fantastic, appropriate
- Accurate park/situation description
- Good visitor experience descriptions
- Clear organization; well organized; flows well
- Plan tied to management issues/concerns; links to GMP and other planning efforts
- Lots of good (implementation) detail
- Recognized need for visitor studies; evaluation was included in the plan

Conversely, the following comments suggest plan elements that needed improvement, listed in order from most to least number of reviewer comments.

- Need better goals; separate goals from recommendations
- Insufficient analysis, connections not clear; rationale for recommendations needs explaining
- Not enough recommendations; recommendations not specific enough
- Better organization
- More on visitors; (needs more/better description of) current visitor experiences

- More detail and specificity; vague language (needs to be clarified)
- Improve appearance; add graphics
- Missing elements
- Recommendations/implementation planning unrealistic, impractical; need to consider costs of recommendations
- More information needed on resources, existing condition
- Need better foundation statements
- Too many themes; themes could apply to any park;
- Too much information; unhelpful information
- Poor/confusing priorities; priorities non-existent
- Poorly written; needs editing

Each of the 14 Parks whose plans were evaluated in this project received data and comments specific to their plan. Overall, the data and comments from this evaluation have been considered by the Park Service for improvement of NPS Long Range Interpretive Planning.

DISCUSSION AND SUGGESTED REFINEMENTS FOR INTERPRETIVE PLANNING PRINCIPLES

This evaluation project employed both quantitative and qualitative methods to explore the effectiveness of National Park Service long-range interpretive plans. Findings suggest that some plans evaluated were organized, readable, and projected to be useful. Many contained solid foundational elements and reasonable goals and themes. Yet, reviewers also suggested that the analysis (rationale and linkages) included in some of the plans could be strengthened, that the goals and recommendations of some of the plans could be clarified, and that details for implementation could be strengthened.

In general, these findings may be useful for others interested in interpretive planning. As Merritt and Garvin suggest, *"There are many different 'right' ways to plan."*[4] Good planning, guided by basic planning theory, simply describes the process of making clear, disciplined, deliberate, and defensible decisions. Interpretive planning is one such series of decisions in a process of developing exemplary informal education. Toward that end, and based on findings of this project, the following refinements to the principles in Figure 1 are proposed by the author.

- EXCELLENT INTERPRETIVE PLANS are grounded in a **sound planning foundation** that sets the context (purpose, background, situation), provides ground rules, and clarifies assumptions for the planning effort.

- EXCELLENT INTERPRETIVE PLANS describe clear **overall planning goals** and, as appropriate, propose **overall theme(s)** to focus the planning effort.

- EXCELLENT INTERPRETIVE PLANS articulate an appropriate **assessment of the current condition** to help the ultimate users of the plan better understand the context for planning. This includes (a) an **organized and comprehensive inventory** of the existing condition(s) plus (b) a **deliberate and logical analysis** (rationale) for linking existing situation with proposed recommendations.

- EXCELLENT INTERPRETIVE PLANS contain **clear and specific goals** related to (a) desirable visitor experiences and (b) specific interpretive/educational media, programs, and facilities. Goals help paint a clear picture of what the planning team hopes to achieve, and they help developers direct their efforts toward important outcomes.

- EXCELLENT INTERPRETIVE PLANS propose **specific, reasonable recommendations** that clearly and logically derive from the overall planning goals, current condition, and analysis. Reasonable recommendations provide sufficient implementation detail for proceeding with design and development.

- EXCELLENT INTERPTIVE PLANS integrate **visitor studies and evaluation** as part of the planning-design-development process.

- EXCELLENT INTERPRETIVE PLANS are **well organized, well written, and professionally presented.** They show clear, logical, and rational connections between foundation elements, goals, current conditions, analysis, and recommendations. Their careful organization and clear writing makes them easier to read and use while their professional presentation (e.g., good design, effective graphics) helps communicate the substance of the plan more effectively.

Notes

1. National Park Service, *Interpretive Planning: Interpretation and Visitor Services Guideline. NPS-6,* (Washington, DC: Department of the Interior, 1996), 4.

2. A form of non-probability sample which is characterized by the use of judgment and de-liberate effort to obtain representative samples by including presumably typical areas or groups in the sample. See Fred N. Kerlinger, *Foundations of Behavioral Research*, (New York: Holt, Rinehart, and Winston, 1986), 120.
3. Researchers for this study were two National Park Service planners, who served as coordi-nators of the project, and the author, who served as an evaluation consultant.
4. Elizabeth E. Merritt and Victoria Garvin, *Secrets of Institutional Planning*, (Washington, DC: American Association of Museums, 2007), 6.

References

Kerlinger, Fred N. *Foundations of Behavioral Research.* New York: Holt, Rinehart, and Winston, 1986.
Merritt, Elizabeth E. and Victoria Garvin. *Secrets of Institutional Planning.* Washington, DC: American Association of Museums, 2007.
National Park Service. Interpretive Planning: Interpretation and Visitor Services Guideline. NPS-6. Washington, DC: Department of the Interior, 1996.

Marcella Wells, PhD, is President of Wells Resources, Inc, a woman-owned, small business that specializes in interpretive planning, visitor studies, and project man-agement. Wells Resources works with federal, state, and local land management agencies, informal learning settings (museums, nature centers, arboreta), and non-profit organizations as an advocate for the visitor experience.

Comprehensive Interpretive Plans
A Framework of Questions

Marianna Adams and Judy Koke

Abstract   As explored elsewhere in this publication, the purpose of a Comprehensive or Institution-wide Interpretive Plan (CIP) is to define or articulate the intellectual framework that connects the mission of an organization and its collections with the needs and interests of its audiences. In so doing, it should follow that this plan, shaped by the strength of its collections, mission, and core values, should describe the organization's unique role in the life of a community.

The 2005 American Association of Museum's colloquium described a Comprehensive Interpretive Plan (CIP) as a written plan that outlines the messages the museum wants to convey about content, learning, and the role of the museum in its community. Yet, the collected group was unable to articulate the specific components and process of a successful CIP, possibly because the colloquium was somewhat ahead of its time. Although CIPs are still relatively new for museums, interest is growing as evidenced by more conference presentations on the process and benefit of interpretive plans. It stands to reason that over time, as more and more institutions develop CIPs, we will, collectively, create a clearer framework and process. Meanwhile, we are all left with amorphous good intentions, and no straight path. At the moment, we suggest that this path can be illuminated by answering a series of questions — as a small group, as an institution, and/or as an institution in conversation with its communities — in order to articulate the role of your institution in its community's life long learning environment.[1]

Journal of Museum Education, Volume 33, Number 3, Fall 2008, pp. 293–300.

UNIQUE ROLE

What is unique about our institution's mission and collections? What guides our collection policy? What important and relevant ideas and issues are we particularly well positioned to explore and present? What unifies our research, collections and visitor experiences? Why should the public support us?

This discussion is obviously cross-functional—integrating all departments and roles. The heart of a CIP is about connecting collections and ideas, to audiences, and can only be successful if strongly rooted in the collection and organizational mission. At the outset, it is important to be clear and focused on the role of the museum, understanding that how you think about the museum's role should reflect the spirit and passion of the institution. In addition to staff agreement on the museum's role, they should be energized and inspired by the implications that this role will have on their individual practice.

PUBLIC

Who is our public? This seemingly simple question encapsulates a broad and frank discussion: Is the museum really everyone? Should it be? Who are we currently serving well? Who doesn't come? Why not? Of the non visiting public, who do we most want to reach and why?

Again, discussions on this topic need to be iterative and cross-departmental, as individuals with departments often carry surprisingly diverse concepts of who comprises the visiting public and how they benefit from the museum experience.

The process of reaching consensus on this topic affords the museum staff an opportunity to broaden and enrich its perception of current and possible audiences. Typically we think about audiences in demographic terms, particularly the demographics of age (e.g., adults, children), role (e.g., teachers, parents, students), and sometimes race/ethnicity and economic status (e.g., African-American, Hispanic, low-income). Yet, research strongly suggests that demographics explain very little about how and why visitors benefit from museums.[2] Rather, researchers find that psychographic data (e.g., attitudes, interests, prior knowledge and experience, motivations) does a better job of not only explaining differences among visitors, but in informing our decisions about how to create rich and meaningful experiences for them.

For example, the Denver Art Museum studied visitors to better understand their expectations for the visit and the ways that they look at art.[3] They determined two main audiences, Art Novices and Advanced Amateurs. There are clear differences in the expectations between the two groups. For instance, Novices see the social experience as either the focus of their museum visit or the best way to view art. In contrast, Amateurs tend to prefer viewing on their own, even though they might come to the museum with others. Differences in ways of looking between the two groups were equally marked. For example, Novices tend to be more reactive in that they hope art will "knock them out" and they value feelings from a work of art over the intellectual analysis. This group rarely talks about taking an active role in art viewing. Conversely, the Amateur group tends to engage in more focused or discovery looking by comparing and contrasting or looking intensely. While this group values the emotional experience in art looking they are more comfortable with the intellectual analysis of works of art.

The implications of incorporating a psychographic-based approach to audiences means that exhibitions and programs are responsive to the ways different types of visitors approach and make meaning in the museum. For example, family visitors are not a monolithic audience. Families that are frequent visitors to the museum are more comfortable navigating the space and are more willing to explore on their own. On the other hand, families who do not typically visit the museum often or at all, need more advance organizers.

COMMUNITY NEEDS

Why do people visit our museum? What needs and interests do our target audiences, current and future, have that we are uniquely in a position to respond to?

Frankly, people can live a full and satisfying life and never set foot in a museum. So why do they come?

Jay Rounds suggests that "Visitors come to museums for their own reasons, and those reasons are not necessarily congruent with the goals of the museum."[4] One of their goals is to stabilize and reconfirm a sense of self and the museum is an excellent place to provide a sense of continuity. In addition, museums allow us to explore other ways of being and thinking which often appears as a process of collecting "useless" knowledge, following a relatively random agenda that is driven by what is interesting. This browsing,

Rounds claims, serves as an unconscious preparation for the eventuality that we may need to revise or transform our sense of self in the future.

The days of just putting objects on display or creating interactive experiences that teach aspects of science, art, or history, are over. The museum must be more attuned to how communities are shifting and changing. Our cities are experiencing seismic redistributions of populations. For example, 50% of Toronto citizens were born in another country. This change has major implications for how a museum becomes meaningful to people.

RELATIONSHIP

What is our relationship with our community and what new relationships do we wish to develop? How are we relevant to and perceived in our community? Is it in alignment with how we hope to be perceived? What types of changes are necessary, in the public's eyes, to move from current to desired perception? How important is it that our community understands our purpose and mission? Is it realistic to expect that the community see us as we see ourselves?

Related to personal identity work described above is the work that a community does to support itself as a whole. Museums can play an important part in forming community identity. More than repositories of knowledge and objects, museums are shifting to creating an environment where ideas are explored and meaning is made. They are becoming more transparent about their participation as the arbiters of power and value. This can only be done with successful community participation; the community will only participate if they feel the issues and ideas are interesting and relevant to their everyday lives.

For example, the Ogden Museum of Southern Art in New Orleans found itself playing an important role in the community after the devastation of hurricane Katrina.[5] As the only museum that did not suffer substantial damage, it was able to open soon after the storm. The institution served as both a respite from the grim day-to-day realities of rebuilding by offering exhibitions and social events, and a community forum where citizens could formally and informally debate the relative merits of various rebuilding proposals. It was seen as a physically and psychologically safe space.

This kind of discussion is essentially about the "posture" of the institution. Do we perceive ourselves as the expert and disseminator of information? Do we see ourselves as the facilitator of explorations of particular ideas? Is our role to be the facilitator of conversations, which might end in unexpected places? Each of these "postures" necessitates different program designs. For example, round-table discussions vs. lectures, exhibitions where the primary gateway to meaning is written text vs. opportunities for visitors explore and discover learning on their own through a variety of modalities, and on-site vs. outreach programs.

INTERNAL ALIGNMENT

How will all areas of the museum (retail, marketing, exhibitions, programs, collections and research) pull in the same direction? How do we align the goals and purposes of various departments into clear, coherent messages for greatest impact? How does this direction or message align with our mission and other policies? How can the Board of Trustees be included in the process to assure their support?

This is perhaps the most challenging part of creating a useful and workable interpretive plan. Yet, without internal alignment the museum will be a wagon pulled in different directions, going nowhere. As people become more and more suspicious of media advertising that pushes empty promises, museums need to focus on how the museum can provide a genuine and personally meaningful experience. As Falk and Sheppard point out, "museums have tried too hard to be all things to all people" and not been successful.[6] In the current economic climate, museums must avoid sending mixed messages and be passionately clear about the value of the museum experience. For example, the marketing focus of the museum shop and the conservation message from the curatorial area must not be at odds.

DEFINITION OF SUCCESS

What are the criteria for success? How can we tell if we are accomplishing what we set out to do? What are the priority action steps that move the organization towards it goals? What is a reasonable timeline for accomplishing our objectives?

Traditionally, our organizations measure success by attendance and membership numbers, or even in terms of jobs, and impact on tourism and money into community. More recently, the field has come to understand that exhibition and program evaluation needs to assess how visitors benefit from the experience rather than just count admission receipts, attendance figures, or outputs like number of catalogues printed or programs implemented. Evaluating how well we are doing demands that we listen to visitors and have meaningful conversations with them about their experiences rather than quiz them on the extent to which they ingested specific facts or ideas.

Beyond individual exhibition and program evaluation how will we understand our organization's impact on the community? This most difficult question came into focus for the field with Mark Moore's *Public Value*[7] and has recently been explored in AAM presentations and *Curator* articles by authors such as Korn, Falk, Koster, and others.

CONCLUSION

In working through these questions, institutions begin the challenging job of clarifying their roles for themselves and their publics. The resulting framework can act as a filter for decision making around public offerings and marketing campaigns, for example, as illustrated in the case studies that follow in this issue. A work-in-progress, the written document will require frequent reassessment and revision, as our roles, audiences, and community needs change and evolve. At all stages of development, museum staff must keep in mind how it wants to use the CIP to inform and guide individual and collective practice. No matter how brilliantly written, unless a CIP is frequently used and revised, it becomes a stale and lifeless piece of paper. Over time, the field will develop a more specific understanding of the content, benefits, and process for developing a CIP. Perhaps we could reconvene in 2015 and finish what AAM started in 2005.

Notes

1. Note: These question topics were originally developed by Scott Eberle, Anil Swarupa, Sonal Bhatt, and Judy Koke for an AAM 2007 Annual Conference presentation. The authors have further developed and added to the original presentation.
2. John Falk, "A Framework for Diversifying Museum Audiences: Putting Heart and Head in the Right Place." *Museum News* 77, no 5 (September/October 1998): 36-39.
3. M. McDermott-Lewis, "Through their Eyes: Novices and Advanced Amateurs," The Denver Art Museum Interpretive Project (1990): 7–46, http://www.denverartmuseum.org/discover_the_dam/museum_resources.
4. Jay Rounds, "Doing Identity Work in Museums," *Curator* 49, no. 2, (April 2006): 132–150.
5. Presentation by Kate Barron, Education Coordinator, Ogden Museum of Southern Art, at the National Art Education Association Museum Education Pre-Conference (March 2008).
6. John H. Falk & Beverly K. Sheppard, *Thriving in the Knowledge Age* (Lanham, MD: AltaMira, 2006).
7. Mark Moore, *Creating Public Value* (Cambridge, MA: Harvard University, 1997).

Marianna Adams is president of Audience Focus, Inc. which supports museums, cultural organizations, and other informal learning environments in the development of unique life-enriching experiences for diverse audiences. Dr. Adams specializes in professional development for museum practitioners to learn how to conduct their own evaluation, in designing visitor studies that assist museums in better understanding and service audiences, and in facilitating interpretive planning efforts at museums. She can be contacted at Marianna@audiencefocus.com.

Judy Koke is the Deputy Director of Education and Public Programming for the Art Gallery of Ontario in Toronto, Canada. In this capacity she leads the interpretive planning and visitor research functions for the museum. Formerly a Senior Researcher at the Institute for Learning Innovation, she has extensive background in research and evaluation and in integrating visitor input into museum planning. Previously, the in-house evaluator at the Denver Museum of Nature and Science for six years, Judy was later the Assistant Director of the University of Colorado Museum of Natural History. She has taught in several graduate Museum Studies Programs and has published widely on youth programs, gender differences in science attitudes and specific audience segments.

Just Do It

Resources for Interpretive Planning

Jes Koepfler

Abstract   Now that you have finished reading this journal issue and understand what interpretive planning is and when to apply it, how can you get started and just *do* it? This article provides an annotated list of practical handbooks and internet resources that provide guidelines for museum practitioners to engage in interpretive planning at institutions ranging from art museums to science centers to national parks.

The aim of this resource section is to provide professionals, who have just read this edition of the journal, with the answer to the question, "Now that I understand what interpretive planning is, how do I get started at my institution?" The bibliographies and content of the previous articles and case studies cover the theory of interpretive planning and the range of its definitions. This article will not reiterate those resources, nor the resources of other associated lists such as the one in "Civic Discourse: Let's Talk".[1] Instead this list suggests a number of practical handbooks and internet resources that provide step-by-step suggestions for how to engage in interpretive planning at institutions ranging from art museums to national parks. This list is by no means exhaustive but serves as a useful starting point in the implementation of interpretive planning strategies. Titles are listed in alphabetical order by citation for each section.

HANDBOOKS AND HOW-TOS

Ambrose, Timothy, and Crispin Paine. *Museum Basics.* Second edition. Units 14-16 and 22-27. New York: Routledge, 2006. ISBN 0-415-36633-X

   Museum Basics, second edition, by Timothy Ambrose and Crispin Paine,

Journal of Museum Education, Volume 33, Number 3, Fall 2008, pp. 301–308.

provides a number of units related to museum learning and interpretation techniques. Units 14-16 briefly address learning in museums and museum education services inside and outside the museum, while Units 22-27 cover interpretation, presentation techniques for interactive and visitor-oriented displays, and also the more technical aspects of lighting to inform exhibition practices related to engaging and communicating with visitors. These units are written simply and plainly as a basic guide to all aspects of audience development and education for any institution.

"New Technologies as Part of a Comprehensive Interpretive Plan," by Peter Samis
"Technology's No Tea Party for Small Museums," by Angela Spinazze
"Analyzing Return on Investment: Process of Champions," by Leonard Steinbach
Din, Herminia, and Hecht, Phyllis (eds.). *The Digital Museum: A Think Guide*. Washington, DC: American Association of Museums, 2007. ISBN-13: 978-1-933253-09-1

Interpretive planning is being shaped partly by the shift from the Industrial Age to the Information Age. *The Digital Museum: A Think Guide*, edited by Herminia Din and Phyllis Hecht, published in cooperation with the Media and Technology Standing Professional Committee of the American Association of Museums, invites practitioners at all levels of interpretive planning--from within IT departments, to education divisions, consulting, and more--to consider how and when information technology can (or should) be incorporated into the museum. Given the anxiety associated with the pace of technological change for museums, all chapters are a valuable read; however, individuals engaged specifically in interpretive planning may want to turn their attention in particular to the following chapters, which provide thoughtful discussion, questions to consider, and new models for decision-making:

Edson, Gary and David Dean. *The Handbook for Museums*. Chapters 10-12. New York: Routledge, first published 1994, reprinted 2003. ISBN 0-415-09953-6

Gary Edson and David Dean offer three chapters in *The Handbook for Museums*, which cover interpretation in general, object interpretation specifically, and museum education as a whole in a succinct and easy-to-follow layout. Each chapter contains a discussion of the topic with associated models and charts for quick access as well as interesting quotes to engage the reader. First published in 1994, the book was reprinted in 2003 and contains information relevant to today's needs. However, technological approaches to interpretation are not a primary focus of Edson and Dean's discussion, and other resources, such as *The Digital Museum: A Think Guide* mentioned earlier, should serve to supplement.

Ravelli, Louise J. *Museum Texts: Communication Frameworks*. New York: Routledge, 2006. ISBN 0-415-28430-9

Text is an important medium through which museums communicate to their visitors. Louise J. Ravelli's *Museum Texts: Communication Frameworks* offers examples regarding the appropriate level of complexity for text labels, choices of language, how to represent particular points of view in the content, and more. Ravelli's expertise and interest in the relationship of communication to its social context shines through in this detailed discussion of interpretive texts.

Weaver, Stephanie. *Creating Great Visitor Experiences: A Guide for Museums, Parks, Zoos, Gardens, & Libraries*. Walnut Creek, CA: Left Coast Press, 2007. ISBN 1598741683

Stephanie Weaver's work spans visitor experiences across all cultural heritage institutions. Her handbook-styled reader, *Creating Great Visitor Experiences: A Guide for Museums, Parks, Zoos, Gardens, & Libraries*, is written specifically with the museum practitioner in mind. It provides checklists and exercises keyed to each chapter along with associated resources and websites to help museum professionals develop more rewarding and welcoming experiences for their visitors. The book provides a flexible, practical framework that one could apply to a small project as easily as to a program overhaul.

MODELS AND BEST PRACTICES

Black, Graham. Section 4: Planned to Engage: using interpretation to develop museum displays and associated service. In *The Engaging Museum: Developing Museums for Visitor Involvement*. New York: Routledge, 2005. ISBN 0-415-34557-X

In Section 4 of *The Engaging Museum: Developing Museums for Visitor Involvement*, author Graham Black draws on his own experience and that of others to examine the role of effective interpretation in museum displays. He provides an easy-to-use format with chapter introductions and discussion sections, relevant case studies to illustrate where theory meets practice, and models, tables, and planning suggestions to guide exhibition development.

Brochu, Lisa. *Interpretive Planning: The 5-M Model for Successful Planning Projects.* Fort Collins, CO: The National Association for Interpretation, 2003. ISBN-10: 1879931125

Lisa Brochu is a Certified Interpretive Planner and works for the National Association for Interpretation. Her book, *Interpretive Planning: The 5-M Model for Successful Planning Projects,* is designed for informal environmental education but provides sound, practical advice applicable to all museum professionals. The 5-M Model covers management, message, market, mechanics, and media as a "common sense way to remember all the considerations that should affect the decision-making process" in an interpretive plan.

Falk, John H., Lynn D. Dierking, and Susan Foutz, Eds. *In Principle, In Practice: Museums as Learning Institutions.* Part II, Chapters 6-9. Lanham, MD: AltaMira Press, 2007. ISBN-13: 978-0-7591-0977-3, ISBN-10: 0-7591-0977-X

The *In Principle, In Practice* initiative, spear-headed by the Institute for Learning Innovation in Edgewater, Maryland, included a national conference (November 7-8, 2004) as well as a published collection of essays and chapters written by recognized professionals in the field. Edited by John H. Falk, Lynn D. Dierking, and Susan Foutz, essays in Part II: Engaging Audiences in Meaningful Learning cover interpretive planning as it pertains primarily to informal science education but tackles some of the sticky issues of cultural relevance, reflective practice, and issues-based learning, which are applicable and increasingly important for institutions in the 21st century.

Peters, Sarah, Amy P. Brady, Reggie Prim, and Sarah Schultz. "Art and Civic Engagement: Mapping the Connections." In *Expanding the Center: Walker Art Center and Herzog & de Meuron.* Steve Dietz, Robin Dowden, Sarah Schultz, and Richard Flood, Eds. Minneapolis: Walker Art Center, 2005. ISBN 0935640843

The in-depth case study *Expanding the Center: Walker Art Center and Herzog & de Meuron,* describes a pivotal moment in the life cycle of many large museums—expansion. As is the case with many building campaigns, it is not simply the architecture that changes. These transformations also provide an opportunity for institutions to internally restructure their missions and strategic thinking. The chapter on "Art and Civic Engagement: Mapping the Connections" by Sarah Peters, Amy P. Brady, Reggie Prim, and Sarah Schultz, looks at the Walker in this transition period and describes its adoption of the "Town Square" metaphor as an institutional framework. To handle this approach, staff followed a 4C model (container, convener, connector, and catalyst) to help visitors engage in and understand the roles that art and artists play.

INTERNET RESOURCES

N.B. In some cases these resources restrict access to members only.

American Association of Museums, www.aam-us.org

The American Association of Museums and other similar professional organizations across the world offer a wealth of online materials for interpretive planning. The AAM's National Interpretation Project initiative puts together a number of resources online and in print. Every other year they provide a professional development workshop that addresses current issues for museum educators. For example, this year's Learning in Museums Seminar focused on "Technology, Interpretation and Learning in Museums". In many cases, an associated publication and online write-up results from these meetings and can be accessed through AAM's website by typing "LiM" into the Search box.

ExhibitFiles, www.exhibitfiles.org

ExhibitFiles, developed by the Association of Science-Technology Centers and funded by the National Science Foundation, is an invaluable resource that is rich in content, easily navigated, and, unlike most other web resources in its type, amount of content currently available to museum practitioners. It is an online community of exhibit designers and developers building a shared collection of exhibition records and personal reviews. While it is not specifically driven by interpretive planning needs, the site offers insights from members in the field and a wealth of information and images on past and recent exhibitions. As a result, the site, which recently won Best of the Web 2008 in the Professional category, will help professionals achieve successes and avoid failures.

Museums Australia, www.museumsaustralia.org.au

Museums Australia (WA), in joint publication with the National Trust of Australia (WA), offers, among other resources, a recent publication in PDF format called *Sharing Our Stories: Guidelines for Heritage Interpretation* (2007). This document covers everything from definitions of interpretation and heritage to securing funding for interpretive plans. The PDF is most easily reached through this link at the National Trust in Western Australia Web site: http://www.ntwa.com.au/SHARE_REPORT_2007_email_RGB.pdf.

Museums, Libraries and Archives Council, www.museums.gov.uk

The Museums, Libraries and Archives Council, which replaced the Museums and Galleries Commission, provides policies, programs, and publications "to raise professional standards and champion better services for users and readers of all ages and backgrounds" in England. A wealth of resources relevant to learning and planning for inclusion, digital technology, and more, can be found under the "Policy," "Programmes," and "Publications" tabs. The site also provides its empirical research and evaluation studies for practitioners to draw upon.

National Association for Interpretation, www.interpnet.com

The National Association for Interpretation offers certification, training, and resources for interpretive planners in the United States, Canada, and other countries around the world. In addition to their consulting services, they also produce publications such as *The Interpreter*, *Journal of Interpretation Research*, and *Legacy Magazine*. Its mission is to inspire leadership and excellence to advance heritage interpretation as a profession.

National Park Service. Interpretative Media Selection. 2004, http://www.nps.gov/hfc/products/ip.htm

The National Park Service is well known for its focus on visitors and interpretation techniques. It has a wealth of resources on its various web sites. The Harpers Ferry Center in particular has been providing the National Park Service with interpretive planning strategies and expertise for over 30 years. The site offers guidelines for funding sources and point-by-point descriptions to help practitioners select interpretive media.

Scottish Museums Council, www.scottishmuseums.org.uk

The Scottish Museums Council provides fact sheets as useful resources including the "Introduction to Interpretive Planning" and "Planning for Effective Interpretive Planning" (2003). These documents outline the who, what, when, where, and why of interpretive planning and are geared towards those new to or less familiar with the process.

ACKNOWLEDGMENTS

I would like to acknowledge Judy Koke (editor of this issue and Deputy Director of Education at the Art Gallery of Ontario, Toronto, Canada) and Cheryl Meszaros (author in this issue and Lecturer in the Museum Studies program, Faculty of Information, University of Toronto, Canada) for their assistance and direction in developing this resource list. I would also like to extend my thanks to Nick Gamble, a friend and colleague, who assisted with the clarity of this piece.

Notes

1. *Museums & Social Issues,* **V**ol. 2, no. 2, (Fall 2007).

Jes Koepfler is a research associate at the Institute for Learning Innovation, a non-profit informal education research and evaluation organization based in Maryland. She has a varied background in museum studies, new media, and classical archaeology. Her current research interests include investigating the effectiveness and appropriateness of technology components for visitors in informal learning institutions, as well as the value and dissemination of open source software applications to non-profits for project management and development.